ALAN E. NOURSE, M.D.

AIDS

REVISED EDITION
FRANKLIN WATTS
NEW YORK   LONDON   TORONTO   SYDNEY
1989

Library of Congress Cataloging-in-Publication Data

Nourse, Alan Edward.
    AIDS / Alan E. Nourse. — Rev. ed.
        p.   cm.
    Bibliography: p.
    Includes index.
    Summary: Discusses the possible origins, symptoms, and characteristics
of AIDS, the ongoing search for a cure, and myths and fears concerning the
epidemic.
    ISBN 0-531-10662-4
    1. AIDS (Disease)—Juvenile literature. [1. AIDS (Disease)]
I. Title.
RC607.A26N68   1989
616.97'92—dc 19   88-30381   CIP   AC

CONTENTS

CHAPTER ONE

BEGINNINGS

Exactly when and where and how it first began, nobody knows. We may never know for sure. The first cases may have occurred as many as twenty or thirty years ago, but probably not much before. Almost certainly it went unrecognized at first. The earliest tragic victims simply sickened and died for no apparent reason, without any idea what was wrong with them.

As to where and how it began, we can only make some educated guesses. From the few clues we have, it seems possible that a simple virus, which had been living more or less harmlessly in the bodies of certain gray-green African monkeys for many years, suddenly underwent a spontaneous internal change or mutation that altered its behavior slightly—but significantly. Before this change, that virus—nothing more than a tiny bundle of nucleic acid wrapped up in a protein envelope—might not have been able to survive anywhere except in the bodies of that particular species of monkey. Although infected members of that monkey tribe might well have come into contact with human beings now and then, humans had never been infected by the virus. The mutation or change that occurred in the virus probably didn't amount to much in terms of its structure—maybe nothing more than a shifting around of a few molecules in its central nucleic acid chain. But even that simple change had terrible consequences, because suddenly the mutated virus could attack and infect human beings as well as monkeys.

We can imagine that at some time, perhaps twenty or thirty years ago, a wandering tribesman in some remote area of hot central Africa came in contact with that changed virus and became infected. Maybe he tried to capture a gray-green monkey and it bit him. Maybe he killed it for food and came in contact with its blood. Whatever the incident, it must have been so minor that the man forgot about it within a day or so. And nothing terrible happened for days, weeks, maybe even months—until one day, for reasons he couldn't guess, he started to get sick.

He began running fevers and losing weight. Suddenly he was terribly tired all the time. Strange swellings appeared in his neck and under his arms. Somehow that changed virus, reproducing in his body, began causing serious damage. At the same time, that virus began appearing in his bloodstream and semen. Without any idea of what was happening, the man passed the virus on to his wife during sexual intercourse, and soon she, too, began to sicken. The baby she was carrying died within a few days after being born, and she and the man both died soon after.

Meanwhile, we can imagine that other men and women in the area suffered accidental contact with infected monkeys and became sick themselves. Possibly the accepted sexual practices of those remote country people contributed more than anything else to the spread of the infection from person to person and from village to village, either through everyday, ordinary sexual contacts or at special feast times when there was great intermixing of the sexes and widespread sexual contact. Because, unknown to them, the deadly virus was spread from person to person more easily by sexual contact than any other way.

Thus, within perhaps two or three years after the first case appeared, a dozen other men and women had sickened and died from the mysterious "fever disease" and a hundred more in the area were already fatally infected. Some of those people moved on to the cities to infect others, and some in the cities who became infected went on to other countries. Many of these people were already dreadfully ill, and many more who were infected would soon become sick. Only the deadly virus was alive and well, and from some such simple beginnings, a deadly human plague was born.

A MODERN PLAGUE

Nobody knows for sure that this is really how the disease we call AIDS got started; it's just one theory that doctors think is possible. Nor do we know exactly when or how it first came to America. But we do know that somehow a modern-day plague got started quite recently, probably somewhere in central Africa, and began spreading. During the past eight years we have been watching that plague grow and evolve before our very eyes into a full-blown nightmare in the United States and throughout the world. The first isolated cases of AIDS probably appeared in our country as early as 1968 or 1969 and went unrecognized until years later. It wasn't until the summer of 1981 that clusters of cases began to appear, and our medical scientists realized that something very strange and unpleasant was afoot. In that year approximately 150 cases of AIDS were diagnosed, and some 30 people died from the disease.

That was just the beginning. By January 16, 1989, according to the latest available official reports, more than eighty-four thousand (84,133) cases of AIDS had been reported in the United States alone, and over forty-seven thousand (47,049) of those people had already died. Even more grim, very few people known to have developed the full-blown disease had survived much longer than three years. When all the official figures are in for 1987, it is believed that some twenty-eight thousand new cases will have been diagnosed in that one year alone in the United States, with over twelve thousand deaths from the disease during 1987. And these figures are expected to double in the course of 1988. In fact, the Centers for Disease Control (CDC) in Atlanta, Georgia—our national public health authority on AIDS—projects that by the end of 1992, AIDS cases in the United States will total approximately 365,000, with a cumulative death toll of 263,000. For 1992 *alone* the estimates are 80,000 new cases diagnosed.*

At the time this book is being written, there is no known way to prevent the virus from infecting anyone

---

*Centers for Disease Control.

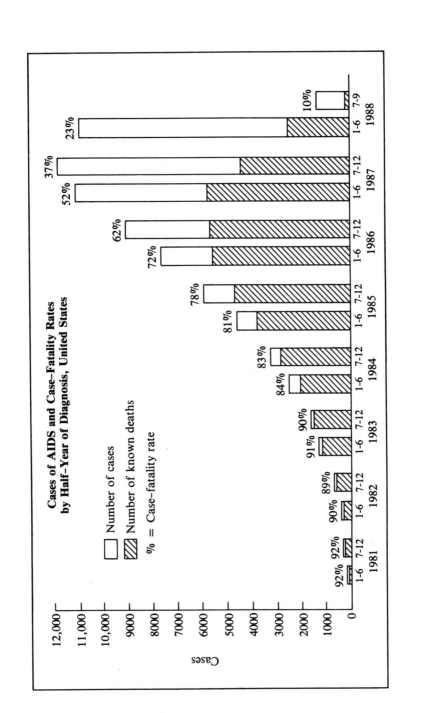

Cases of AIDS and Case–Fatality Rates
by Half–Year of Diagnosis, United States

who is exposed to it through intimate contact (we will explain later exactly what is meant by "intimate contact") and although treatment may extend the lives of some victims for a while, there is no cure for the disease. It is likely that the vast majority of those who have the full-blown disease today are going to die from its effects sooner or later. Based upon what is now known about the disease, one authority on AIDS speculates that approximately one-half of some five hundred thousand male homosexuals in the greater New York City area alone already harbor the virus in their bodies. The CDC currently estimates that in the entire country as many as one and a half million people may already have been infected,* and most scientists now think that 50 percent or more of those people will eventually develop the full-blown, lethal form of the disease. Indeed, many of the scientists who know the most about AIDS believe that these figures may actually be underestimates. Probably all that we have seen of this disease so far is the tip of the iceberg.

THE PEOPLE AT RISK

During the past eight years AIDS has become the subject of one of the most intense emergency research efforts in all medical history. The figures, of course, explain why. An enormous amount has been learned about the disease in a very short time, and the story of this period of research and discovery is both fascinating and frightening.

---

*Centers for Disease Control. *Morbidity and Mortality Weekly Report,* Vol. 36, No. 49. December 18, 1987.

Among other things, scientists have learned that some of the early ideas about what caused the disease and who was in danger of getting it were either completely wrong or else no longer apply. At first the disease seemed to attack only individuals in a few sharply limited minority groups: male homosexuals, for example, or people who were users of illicit intravenous drugs (people shooting up heroin, for instance); people who had recently come to the United States from Haiti; or people who suffered from the rare blood-clotting disease known as hemophilia. So many of those early cases were male homosexuals, for instance, that people began thinking and speaking of the disease as "The Gay Plague." And it was believed, at first, that people who were not members of these small, limited minority groups were completely safe from the disease.

The evolving facts soon began to contradict these ideas. It quickly became clear, for example, that babies were developing AIDS and dying in the first or second year of life. A few school-age children were coming down with it, all of them recipients of infected blood products through transfusions required by hemophilia or other illnesses. And it became evident that a small but growing number of both men and women were apparently contracting AIDS through heterosexual (male-female) sex contacts. It was found that both men and women were being affected by the disease on the island of Haiti itself, and that the disease was far more prevalent than previously suspected among both men and women in such central African nations as Zaire, Rwanda, and Burundi, where transmission between men and women during heterosexual contact seemed more common than any other way.

**Reported Adult/Adolescent Cases of AIDS, by Patient Group,
United States, 1981 to October 24, 1988
Total: 75,458**

Patient group:

Homosexual/bisexual male (63%)

IV drug user (19%)

Homosexual male and IV drug abuser (7%)

Hemophilia/coagulation disorder (1%)

Heterosexual cases (4%)

Transfusion, blood/components (3%)

Undetermined (3%)

**Reported Cases of Children with AIDS by Patient Group*,
United States, 1981 to October 24, 1988
Total: 1,212**

Patient group:

Hemophilia/coagulation disorder (6%)

Parent with/at risk of AIDS (78%)

Transfusion, blood/components (13%)

Undetermined (3%)

*Includes all patients under 13 years of age
at time of diagnosis.

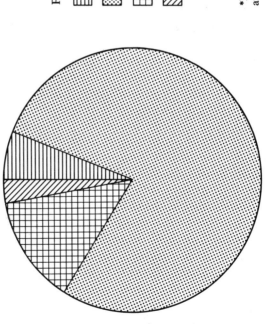

Indeed, many doctors who know the most about the disease today recognize that male-to-female or female-to-male sexual transmission of AIDS in the United States does indeed occur, and will continue to increase among heterosexuals, however slowly. And if so, then it may soon be that almost nobody will be completely outside the reach of this deadly virus, no matter what their sexual preferences and practices.

A DEADLY PATTERN

Today we know that AIDS is caused by a virus that invades the blood and other body fluids of the infected person, and is primarily transmitted by sexual contact, by contact with contaminated blood or blood products, or by an infected mother to her unborn baby through the placenta. But what does this virus do to the human body that is so deadly and different from all other viruses? Of course we know that other viruses can kill people, too, and that different viruses do their damage in many different ways. Some, like the recently conquered smallpox virus, damaged many different tissues throughout the body and led to death through a massive viremia, or virus blood poisoning. The rabies virus kills by relentlessly attacking and destroying just one particular kind of tissue—the nerve cells in the brain and spinal cord. The hepatitis B virus can cause death by destroying cells in the liver.

The AIDS virus does its dirty work in a very different way. The virus primarily attacks and destroys certain kinds of white blood cells known as *lymphocytes,* the cells that form the vital foundation of the body's protective immune system. As we will see later, it is this immune system that protects our bodies

18

against all sorts of disease-causing microorganisms with which we are constantly coming in contact. It also helps protect our healthy bodies against the development of certain kinds of malignant tumors or cancers. We depend upon the body's immune system for our very lives from the time we are born to the time we die.

The AIDS virus, once introduced into the body, begins to destroy those very special kinds of lymphocyte cells that we depend upon the most to make the body's immune system work. Within a short time the infected individual becomes *immune-deficient*—that is to say, his or her immune protective system begins to work less efficiently—and this immune deficiency grows progressively worse and worse. Scientists speak of this kind of immune deficiency as *acquired,* or picked up from outside the body, to distinguish it from other immune deficiencies that we know are inborn or inherited in the individual's genes. Then, as the immune system caves in more and more, the infected person begins to develop a *syndrome,* a characteristic group of symptoms, that seems to appear as a direct result of the immune deficiency. It is this deadly pattern of events that explains the name given to this disease: *A*cquired *I*mmune *D*eficiency *S*yndrome, or simply AIDS.

The early symptoms that begin to appear as a part of this syndrome often seem very vague and mysterious. The person may begin running daily fevers, or perspiring heavily at night. This may be accompanied by a marked weight loss. Sometimes there is a swelling of lymph nodes, small glandlike clusters of lymphocytes located in the neck, under the arms, in the groin, and in other parts of the body. In some cases intestinal disturbances such as nausea, cramps, or diarrhea begin to occur.

Then, as the immune deficiency becomes worse, the disease can take a second and more ominous turn. The person starts coming down with one or another of a variety of strange infections caused by microorganisms that practically never cause infections in healthy human beings because the healthy person's immune system slaps them down before they ever have a chance to get started. Some people also begin developing certain very unusual kinds of cancers that rarely appear in normal younger people because the healthy immune system usually manages to fight them off. These infections and cancers often prove extremely difficult to treat effectively, and even when treatment seems to help, they tend to come right back again as soon as treatment is ended. The unfortunate person with this pattern of illness, now spoken of as "full-blown AIDS," may spend months or years going from one serious infection to another, one crisis to another, and will ultimately die when one of these infections or cancers no longer responds to any treatment and finally overwhelms all defenses.

A MODERN CHALLENGE

Obviously such a disease, caused and spread by a virus that is running rampant, poses a dreadful danger. And so far almost everything that has been learned about this disease has been bad. So far scientists have found no effective way to attack and kill the virus in a victim's body. Newly discovered drugs may slow down its deadly activity for a while, but no drug yet can cure the disease. From experience with multitudes of cases, it has become clear that once the immune system has been damaged by this virus, it never gets better. No treatment has been found to help the immune system recover. AIDS researchers agree that the very best hope for the future would be a vaccine that could be used before exposure, to prevent infection by the virus—but no such vaccine has been yet been found to be safe and effective, in spite of the best efforts of the many brilliant scientific minds working on the problem.

This means that *prevention* of the infection in the first place is the greatest and most immediate challenge facing us today. And since many people in all walks of life are at risk of contracting the infection, or very soon may be, it is vital that everyone know some basic facts about this disease: where it comes from, what it can do to a person, and what patterns of living can offer people the best chances for avoiding it. At the same time, it is equally important that the false ideas and groundless fears about the disease which have arisen in people's minds be dispelled, so that nobody is needlessly hurt while research for its prevention and cure goes on.

The best place to begin looking for the facts about AIDS is its first recognized appearance in this country just a few short years ago as a mysterious and deadly plague which nobody could make any sense of.

CHAPTER TWO

A DEADLY SYNDROME

The young man in the hospital bed was terribly ill, there was no question about that. The trouble was that none of the doctors treating him could figure out exactly how or why he was ill, and nothing they did for him seemed to help in the slightest.

The time was early 1981, the patient a successful thirty-one-year-old artist who had never been sick in his life before he turned up at this large medical school hospital in Los Angeles. The problem that brought him there was very strange. He was suffering from a yeast infection known as candidiasis, more commonly known as "thrush," which had attacked his throat and esophagus so severely that he could hardly breathe or swallow. The odd thing was that yeast infections due to the organism known as *Candida albicans,* although fairly common in a milder form in newborn babies before their immune systems have had time to fully mature, were practically never seen in healthy adults. The only adults who ever appeared with this kind of severe *Candida* infection were patients whose immune systems had been deliberately suppressed by medication—following a kidney transplant operation, for instance—or who were badly beaten down by certain kinds of cancer. When this young man's immune system was investigated by laboratory tests, his doctors discovered that a particular kind of lymphocyte white blood cell which would normally protect a healthy adult from *Candida* infections was almost completely absent from his bloodstream. Unlikely as it seemed, his doctors concluded that he must have some rare form of blood cancer, or leukemia.

The doctors treated his infection, and after a few weeks he had recovered enough to go home from the hospital. Within a few days he was back again, this time with a severe and rapidly progressing case of pneumonia. But the pneumonia was *not* due to a recurrence of the *Candida* infection. Instead, the young man's lungs were now filled with a rare one-celled protozoan organism known as *Pneumocystis carinii,* which causes a singularly deadly form of pneumonia known to attack only people who had terribly deficient immune systems. While they tried desperately to treat the pneumonia with drugs they hoped might turn the infection, the young man grew sicker and sicker and finally died. And the doctors were left with an unanswered question: Why had this previously healthy young man suddenly developed these two strange infections? It seemed that his immune system had simply caved in—but why?

Shortly after that patient's death another young man was admitted to the same hospital with an equally bizarre collection of symptoms. Like the first patient, this man was in his early thirties, and like the first patient, he was homosexual. But this man had already been sick at home for months, spiking fevers up to 104°F (40°C) every day, sweating profusely at night, and losing over 30 pounds (14 kg) of weight. The cases were different in other ways, too. The doctors who examined this man found swollen lymph nodes in his neck and under his arms. Routine lab tests revealed no explanation for this strange pattern of symptoms, but when his doctors looked closely at his immune protective system they discovered that he, too, had an inexplicable absence of T-helper lymphocytes in his bloodstream—the kind of white blood cells the body depends upon for immune protection against a wide variety of infections.

Within a matter of days a third young man turned up at the same hospital with a severe case of *Pneumocystis carinii* pneumonia. Like the other two men, this man was homosexual, and like the others, he had frequented homosexual bathhouses patronized by many young homosexual men in the Los Angeles area. What was more, this man was also a user of illicit intravenous drugs and had frequently shared hypodermic needles and other injection equipment with other drug users. He even showed evidence of previous infection with hepatitis B, a serious virus infection of the liver often contracted from the use of contaminated hypodermic needles. In addition, his doctors found that he was infected with one of the herpes viruses known as cytomegalovirus, or CMV, a kind of infection known to be shared by many homosexual men.

A COMMON THREAD

We know that medical history over the years is filled with isolated cases of strange and inexplicable diseases. Over twelve years earlier, for example, a sixteen-year-

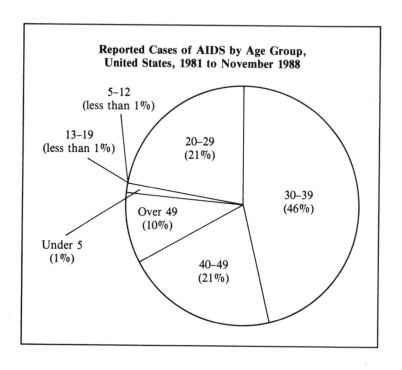

Reported Cases of AIDS by Age Group, United States, 1981 to November 1988

5–12 (less than 1%)

13–19 (less than 1%)

20–29 (21%)

30–39 (46%)

Over 49 (10%)

Under 5 (1%)

40–49 (21%)

old boy had sickened and died from an illness so baffling that his doctors had actually frozen and saved some of his blood in hope that later research might reveal the cause of his death. (Only later was it shown that he had died of AIDS). But it was clear to the doctors treating these three young men that theirs were not exactly isolated cases. True enough, the patients didn't know each other and had never had direct contact with each other—but there was a common thread connecting them. All three were homosexual. All three frequented homosexual bathhouses and gave histories of frequent and repeated sexual contacts with large numbers of other homosexual men over a period of months before becoming ill. These homosexual contacts often involved anal intercourse (intercourse in which the man's penis is inserted into the partner's rectum as part of the sex act). All three of these patients had been found to have a severe and unexplained deficit in their immune systems that had left them vulnerable to different kinds of so-called *opportunistic infections*—infections that only occur when an impaired immune system gives them an opportunity to take hold, and thus practically never occur in people with healthy, normal immune systems.

Soon these patients proved not to be "isolated cases" for yet another reason. As 1981 wore on, more and more victims of this mysterious syndrome began appearing in the Los Angeles area. Public health officials were notified, and reports of these early cases were sent to the U.S. Public Health Service Centers for Disease Control (CDC), in Atlanta, where they were reported in the weekly publication called *Morbidity and Mortality Weekly Report* in order to alert doctors in other areas of the country to be on the lookout for similar cases.

And similar cases there were. A cluster of six or seven cases appeared among young homosexual men in San Francisco. These cases were singular because one of the patients was found to have had sexual contact with at least five of the others within a brief period of time. Meanwhile, cases began appearing in New York City and Newark, New Jersey. Several of these cases proved to be different from the others in an ominous way: some patients, rather than developing opportunistic infections such as candidiasis or *Pneumocystis carinii* pneumonia, began appearing instead with a form of cancer of the blood vessels in the skin called *Kaposi's sarcoma*—a kind of cancer that had virtually never before appeared in young people and had

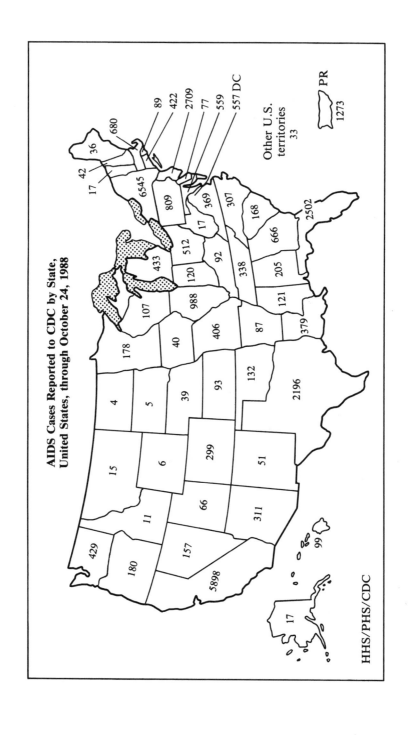

AIDS Cases Reported to CDC by State, United States, through October 24, 1988

89
422
2709
77
559
557 DC

Other U.S. territories
33

PR
1273

680
36
42
17
6545
809
809
17
369
307
168
2502
512
92
666
433
120
338
205
107
988
87
121
406
132
379
178
40
93
2196
39
4
5
51
299
6
15
311
66
11
157
180
429
5898
99
17

HHS/PHS/CDC

formerly been seen only rarely in elderly men with a Mediterranean nationality background. And some of the patients in New York not only developed a virulent and fast-moving form of Kaposi's sarcoma, but came down with opportunistic infections as well. Finally, as the cases in New York, San Francisco, and Los Angeles increased, the city of Miami appeared as a focus of additional cases, and victims were recognized in cities such as Seattle, St. Louis, and Washington, D.C., as well.

In many of these cases the common thread was often broken, or was extremely confusing and difficult to follow. The patients' illnesses were not identical (unlike the smallpox infections that ravaged the American Indians on the western frontier in the mid-1800s, which were almost all identical). Some of these patients had been sick for weeks or months with high fevers, night sweats, diarrhea, or extreme fatigue, before proceeding to a dangerous opportunistic infection. Some had none of these symptoms but reported swelling of lymph nodes for a long period before becoming severely ill. Some developed Kaposi's sarcoma, some developed only opportunistic infections, but some developed both.

Other odd facts began to appear. Although the vast majority of victims in those early cases were male homosexuals, *not all of them were.* Some were totally heterosexual (male-female oriented) in their sexual practices, but were habitual intravenous drug users, and a few wives or consorts of intravenous drug users came down with the syndrome even though they themselves had never used intravenous drugs. A small but distinct percentage of patients did not use intravenous drugs at all, and pursued heterosexual sex lives, but happened to be individuals with a rare blood-clotting disease known as hemophilia, and therefore had had to receive frequent blood transfusions or injections of special blood products in order to keep their blood clotting properly.

But in certain respects the connecting thread was clear and unbroken. Without exception, every one of these desperately ill people had either had prolonged, frequent, intimate contact with other people's bodies through sex relations, or else had had frequent contact with other people's blood or body fluids through blood transfusions or through sharing intravenous drug injection paraphernalia. All of these desperately ill people showed a profound deficiency in their immune systems; and not a single one of them ever got better once they became ill. One by one, their conditions got worse and worse until they died.

During this time another "risk group" appeared. This was a time when many refugees from the island of Haiti were escaping to the United States by boat in a sort of massive emigration, starting in the early 1980s. Most of these people arrived in the Miami area or other areas in the deep South. And soon a small percentage of cases of the new disease was identified in both men and women from Haiti who had arrived in the United States before 1978. Oddly enough, most of these Haitian victims could not be consistently connected either with homosexual activity or with intravenous drug use. Something else seemed to be involved with them. In addition, a small number of newborn babies sickened and died from the affliction in the first few months of life, even though neither their mothers nor fathers seemed to have any evidence of symptoms. And finally, a few American victims of the disease just

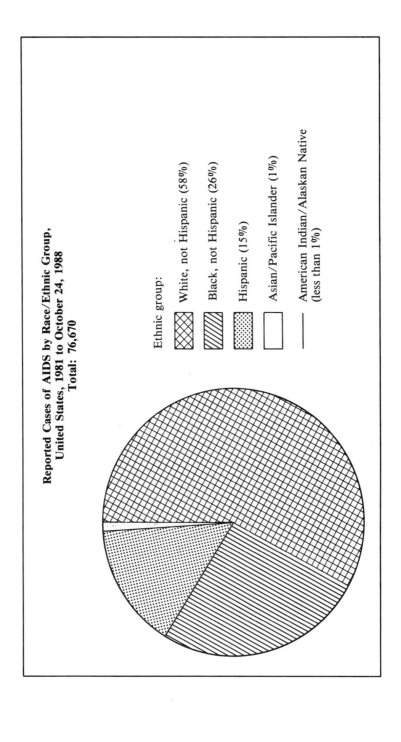

Reported Cases of AIDS by Race/Ethnic Group, United States, 1981 to October 24, 1988
Total: 76,670

Ethnic group:

White, not Hispanic (58%)

Black, not Hispanic (26%)

Hispanic (15%)

Asian/Pacific Islander (1%)

American Indian/Alaskan Native (less than 1%)

didn't match up with *any* of the familiar "risk factors" that seemed to be emerging for the disease: they had never engaged in homosexual activity, they weren't intravenous drug users, they weren't hemophiliacs, they weren't from Haiti, and they weren't newborn babies. But the affliction they had was the same as all the others.

The one common thread among all these emerging cases of deadly illness—the thread that tied every case together—became more and more clear. In every case, without exception, there was a profound immune deficiency that ultimately led to strange and unusual infections or cancers. This immune deficiency had clearly been acquired from some unknown outside source—none of these people had any preexisting, inborn immune deficiency, and none of them had received medicines to depress their immune systems so that transplanted organs might survive. Except in the case of the newborn babies, all of these victims had previously been completely healthy with perfectly normal, intact immune systems. In each case the deadly immune deficiency had been acquired from somewhere else.

THE SEARCH FOR A CAUSE

But acquired from what, and how? What was out there somehow causing this disease to appear? Very early on, public health officials realized that some kind of communicable agent had to be involved—some kind of germ or other microorganism that was being passed from one person to another. The nature of the illness and the apparent pattern of its spread suggested very strongly that the communicable agent was some kind of a virus—not some old, familiar virus that had been hanging around for a long time, but a brand-new virus that nobody had ever heard of before. In certain ways the pattern of spread seemed very similar to that of another well-known virus disease, hepatitis B—a virus that attacked the liver cells and was known to be spread equally well by contaminated needles, contaminated blood products, or sexual contact. And indeed, many of the new victims of AIDS also had hepatitis B infections, or had previously had the disease and recovered, since hepatitis B was so prevalent among sexually active male homosexuals and injectable drug users as well. But clearly the suspected virus could not be just a new form of hepatitis because hepatitis—inflammation of the liver—wasn't one of the features of AIDS, and some AIDS patients had been found by laboratory tests never to have had hepatitis B or any other viral hepatitis at all.

So then what kind of virus was it? What kind of virus might attack only certain kinds of white blood cells—lymphocytes—in the body, and indeed seemed particularly prone to attack just one special family of lymphocytes that had a particular job to do in the body's immune system? Researchers began to speak of this mysterious, unidentified virus as a *lymphotrophic* virus, from Greek words meaning "drawn to the lymph cells." Other researchers called it a *lymphadenopathy* virus because so many victims of AIDS at one time or another developed an "adenopathy," or abnormal glandular swelling, of the lymph glands which contained so many lymphocytes.

All of this led to some interesting speculation. Doctors had known for years about a number of severe cancers of the blood known as leukemias. One of the most common forms of leukemia involves a wild overgrowth of lymphocytes in the bone marrow, where many of them are formed, or in the bloodstream, where they circulate. For many years cancer researchers had suspected that this so-called *lymphocytic leukemia* might actually be caused by some unknown virus. They had known for a long time that viruses were involved in certain kinds of leukemias in chickens, for example, or, more recently, in a kind of leukemia in cats, even though no human leukemia virus had ever been identified. What was more, certain kinds of cancers of the lymph glands, known as lymphomas, were suspected of having a viral origin, since lymphoma viruses had also been identified in several animal species, although never in humans. To many researchers it seemed possible that the unknown AIDS virus might, in fact, be some kind of first cousin to a human leukemia virus, except that instead of forcing lymphocytes to grow and multiply wildly, this virus might just kill lymphocytes, wiping them out altogether.

One scientist who was particularly interested in this question of possible human leukemia viruses was Dr. Robert C. Gallo, head of the Laboratory of Tumor Cell Biology of the National Cancer Institute in Bethesda, Maryland. During the year or so before the first clusters of AIDS cases had come to light, Dr. Gallo and his team had been hot on the trail of one virus they thought might prove to be the cause of a certain rare form of human leukemia. This previously unknown virus seemed to attack the particular kind of lymphocytes known as T-cells (we'll say more about T-cells later) and cause these lymphocytes to grow and reproduce wildly out of control. This had been found to lead to a rare form of blood cancer called *human T-cell leukemia* in a number of people living in southern Japan and in the Caribbean area.

Gallo's research team had called this new virus "human T-cell lymphotropic virus," or HTLV, in the scientific papers they had published describing it. Clearly this virus couldn't be the mysterious cause of AIDS because this virus made human T-lymphocytes suddenly begin reproducing rapidly, thus *increasing* their numbers in the body, whereas the AIDS virus (if there were any such virus) seemed to *destroy* T-lymphocytes. As their search for this mysterious entity went on, yet another human T-cell lymphotropic virus was discovered—similar to the first but not quite the same—which seemed to cause an even rarer form of blood cancer known as *hairy cell leukemia*. Thereafter these two viruses were called HTLV-I and HTLV-II to distinguish them.

With these discoveries, Gallo knew he was getting very close to identifying a similar virus that might be the one that was causing AIDS. Using his experience identifying these other viruses, and working with blood specimens and lymphocyte cell samples taken from AIDS patients, Gallo and his research team finally isolated a third lymphotropic virus, HTLV-III, in the fall of 1982. This virus, unlike the others, *killed* T-cells in the human body instead of goading them on to malignant growth. It appeared that the virus agent causing AIDS had finally been identified.

THREE VIRUSES OR ONE?

Unfortunately, the picture was still not completely clear. While Gallo and his team had been doing their work in the United States, another completely different team of researchers working at the Pasteur Institute in Paris, headed by Dr. Luc Montagnier, announced that *they* had discovered the AIDS virus isolated from a patient suffering from the fevers, night sweats, and swollen lymph glands so typical of the early stages of AIDS. Because the lymphadenopathy was so pronounced in this patient, they named their virus the *lymphadenopathy-associated virus,* or LAV. Then, almost simultaneously, a third virus associated with AIDS patients was announced by an independent team of researchers in San Francisco.

For a while, confusion reigned. It simply didn't make scientific sense that three different viruses could all be involved in a single disease syndrome such as AIDS. And very soon it was shown that there really weren't three different viruses involved after all. Careful study and comparison revealed that Gallo's HTLV-III virus, Montagnier's LAV virus, and the San Francisco virus were all one and the same, either identical to each other or so very nearly so that it was almost impossible to tell them apart. For a while, in some laboratories and publications, the newly discovered AIDS virus was referred to as the HTLV-III/LAV virus. But finally, in 1986, the name-confusion was put to rest. By general consensus, the scientific community agreed to call the virus the *human immunodeficiency virus* or simply HIV, and so it is called today.

With such an important discovery as identifying the AIDS virus, it was perhaps inevitable that a dispute would arise between Gallo's laboratory and Montagnier's team as to who actually discovered it first. For months the press carried accounts of claims, charges, counterclaims, even threatened lawsuits. But today both Gallo and Montagnier agree that credit for the discovery should be equally shared.* Gallo concedes that Montagnier described and identified the HIV virus first, but it was Gallo's team that proved beyond question that that virus was the one that actually caused AIDS. In 1986 Gallo and Montagnier shared the prestigious Lasker Award, the highest scientific honor awarded in North America, for their discovery, and in 1987 they jointly received the Gardner Prize of Canada for their work.

Thus it came about that with an enormous amount of brilliant research, carried out over a very short time, a new killer virus was finally unmasked. But discovering the virus and identifying it in the laboratory were just the first steps in beginning to understand this new plague which has already infected tens of thousands of people in the United States alone and is still spreading with alarming rapidity. To see how such a virus—how *any* virus—could manage to wreak such havoc in so very short a time, we need to pause and consider exactly what viruses are, how they go about causing disease, and how this particular HIV virus and its HTLV cousins can be so different from viruses that cause more benign diseases such as chicken pox or measles.

---

*Gallo, R. C.: Grand Rounds interview with Dennis L. Breo. *American Medical News,* December 4, 1987.

CHAPTER THREE

"A VERY SNEAKY VIRUS INDEED..."

Human beings have been suffering from virus diseases since the dawn of their existence. Viruses have been around on this planet for at least as long as human beings have, and very probably a lot longer. Today we sometimes speak glibly about "virus invaders" and all the trouble they cause when they attack us—but it may, in fact, be closer to the truth to say that *we* are the invaders who have spent most of our existence on earth trying to wrestle control of the planet away from the viruses. If so, we haven't yet even begun to win. The relationship between human beings and viruses goes on today just as it always has: an uneasy relationship at its best, and absolutely disastrous for human beings at its worst.

So what are they, these viruses? And what do they have to do with us?

THE ENEMIES AROUND US

We know that our planet is teeming with life; we are surrounded by living organisms large and small.

Actually, many of the organisms that surround us the most closely and intimately are so tiny that we can't even see them without magnifying lenses, microscopes, or electron beams, and a great many of these so-called *microorganisms* are capable of causing sickness and even death in human beings.

They come in astonishing variety. Among the most familiar are the *bacteria,* tiny single-celled plantlike organisms that can cause such human infectious diseases as tuberculosis, typhoid fever, cholera, and strep throat. Other plantlike organisms known as *yeasts* can cause candidiasis, or thrush, and various kinds of molds and fungi can also invade the body and set up housekeeping.

Other microorganisms are single-celled forms of animal life called *protozoans.* Protozoan organisms can cause such varied diseases as amoebic dysentery, African sleeping sickness, and *Pneumocystis carinii* pneumonia. All the organisms we have mentioned above can live and grow outside the human body as well as inside it, but other organisms such as the *rickettsias,* which cause typhus fever or Rocky Mountain spotted fever, are much smaller and more primitive than even the bacteria, and can only reproduce and multiply inside the bodies of their victims.

Finally, there are the tiniest and most primitive of all the infective microorganisms—the viruses. The simplest and most accurate way to describe a virus is to say that it is nothing more than a long, long molecule of a substance known as *nucleic acid* wrapped up in a special protein envelope. The nucleic acid molecule in a virus is made up of many protein fragments called *amino acids* all bound together in a double spiral form known as DNA (deoxyribonucleic acid) or RNA (ribonucleic acid). We speak of DNA or RNA as "genetic material" because these molecules form the genes in a cell's nucleus that transmit information from one generation of an organism to another, direct what shape the organism can take and what it can do, and thus determine the organism's whole pattern of life. Each different organism's genetic material is very specific for the kind of organism it is. This is why elephants always reproduce more elephants and human beings always reproduce more human beings. And when a virus reproduces, it makes more of the same kind of virus.

A HELPLESS BUT
DANGEROUS FOE

Viruses, however, are very different from other kinds of organisms or microorganisms. Most other microorganisms are perfectly capable of reproducing themselves (given the right conditions of warmth or moisture), taking in nutrients, manufacturing the proteins they need, producing energy, and carrying on all the other normal functions of life without much outside help. But viruses are unable to do *anything* by themselves. They are total parasites. In order to do anything at all, they must first make contact with a living "host" cell and somehow get inside it. Without contact with a living cell the virus—*any* virus—just sits there. Some viruses have even been purified in the form of crystals, as inert as salt crystals in a shaker. In fact, scientists sometimes debate whether viruses deserve to be called "living organisms" at all.

By themselves, viruses are perfectly helpless and harmless. But once a virus comes in contact with the right kind of living cell—say the particular kind of cell in a human being that the virus is capable of invading—it then springs into action in a remarkable way. The protein envelope of the virus particle attaches itself to the outside of the living "host cell" and then literally injects the little packet of virus genetic material directly into the cell. Even there, however, the virus can't do anything for itself. It can't reproduce by itself, for example, because it can't make its own DNA molecule divide into two, and it can't make the protein needed for a new virus particle's protein envelope. Instead, it simply attaches its genetic material—its DNA—onto the DNA in the nucleus of the host cell, and then makes the host cell do all the work.

In a sense the host cell has been captured and enslaved by the virus DNA. Suddenly the host cell finds itself manufacturing carbon copies of the virus's DNA. It also finds itself manufacturing protein envelopes to coat new virus DNA molecules. Within a very short time after the virus has gotten inside the host cell—maybe as little as an hour or two, maybe as long as twenty-four or forty-eight hours—that cell is filled to bursting with the newly formed virus particles it has been forced to manufacture instead of tending to its own business. Finally, having done the virus's dirty work for it, the host cell splits open, releasing dozens or hundreds of new virus particles into the host organism's bloodstream—and then, in most cases, it dies. Meanwhile, each of those new virus particles seeks out another living cell to burrow into and start the whole reproduction process over again.

In truth, all a virus seems to exist for is to find a living host cell of just the right kind and force it to make more viruses. It's just as simple, and seemingly stupid, as that. The virus contributes nothing to the host cell—in fact, in most cases, it ultimately kills it. And although we know of many bacteria that have beneficial effects in the human body (helping us digest our food, for example) or in the outside world (rotting our garbage, turning fallen leaves into soil, and so forth), nobody has ever found a single virus that does anything good for anybody. All it does is force another organism to reproduce it.

HOW VIRUSES BEHAVE

Considering what they are—essentially tiny inert bundles of genetic material wrapped up in protein envelopes—viruses can display some very interesting and complex characteristics once they have found entry into the proper living host cell.

Species specificity. Many viruses seem to be very fussy or specific about which host species they can invade. Dogs don't get head colds or chicken pox (two virus infections that attack human beings quite readily) and human beings don't get distemper. Of all the viruses in the world, there are really only a few that can invade the cells of human beings. Some viruses *do* cross species, however. The rabies virus, for example, can infect dogs, foxes, skunks, even bats, as well as human beings. Researchers suspect that the AIDS virus, HIV, may have originated in monkeys and then altered enough to cross over into human beings—and we now know that the AIDS virus taken from infected human beings can cause an AIDS-like disease in some species of apes and chimpanzees.

Tissue specificity. Among the viruses that do invade human beings, many seem to prefer a certain specific kind of cell to invade. Flu viruses first gain entry into cells in the upper respiratory tract; it is not until they have reproduced in those cells and been released in huge quantities into the bloodstream that the widespread symptoms of typical flu (fever, muscle aches, nausea, and vomiting, among others) appear. The hepatitis B virus attacks liver cells. The polio virus, oddly enough, much prefers cells of the gastrointestinal tract; it is only in exceptional cases that the virus moves on to attack nerve cells in the spinal cord and cause paralysis. Even during the great polio epidemics, most people who were invaded by the polio virus suffered only mild gastrointestinal disturbances before their immune systems got control of the infection. Only an unfortunate few developed paralytic polio.

We know that the HIV virus attacks the body's white blood cells—most particularly the white blood cells known as lymphocytes. There is evidence that this virus attacks, and affects the behavior of, all kinds of lymphocytes in the body, but it seems to do its worst damage in one particular group of lymphocytes, the so-called *T-helper cells*, which we will discuss in more detail a bit later. This virus damages, and then destroys, this particular group of lymphocytes in great numbers—it just kills them—over a prolonged period of time. But it also seems to change the behavior and function of other kinds of lymphocytes in the body at the same time, and even seems to affect other kinds of white cells known as *macrophages* without necessarily killing them.

It is important to bear in mind that many of the worst effects of AIDS on the body arise from this specific action of the virus on the body's lymphocytes.

There is no magic or mystery about it. It happens because it logically has to happen. But we have also learned that this virus can, at the same time, have a dreadful effect on the body's central nervous system. It is not only *lymphotropic,* it is also *neurotropic*—that is, it also attacks and destroys nerve cells in the brain. Scientists today believe that this accounts for the many signs of brain damage, emotional disturbance, or even dementia (mental derangement) that often occur in AIDS patients along with the other physical symptoms.

Selective illness. Another characteristic of many virus invasions of human beings is the odd fact that not everybody infected by a virus necessarily develops the disease that the virus can cause. A normal, healthy immune system is always hard at work trying to fight any virus invasion by producing protective chemicals called *antibodies.* If a person has already been previously infected by a given virus, and still has a horde of antibodies against that virus circulating in the bloodstream, a new attack by the virus might be stopped cold before the virus could gain a new foothold. This is why a person who has once had red measles (or has been vaccinated against it) doesn't ordinarily get red measles again. But even a person without any previous immune protection against a virus may not develop the disease after infection occurs. Even a brand-new immune reaction may be powerful enough to stop the virus in its tracks. In other cases, for reasons unknown, only a few infected people may actually develop symptoms. Some of those who don't get sick may later be found to have antibodies against the virus in their bloodstreams, indicating that the virus has been there—and may well be there still—but no illness ever occurred. And one or two may never show any sign at all of any virus invasion.

The mystery of adaptation. Most viruses that invade human beings sooner or later find a way to adapt to their host—to set up a sort of "peaceful coexistence"— or else the human body learns to adapt to the virus, whichever way you want to look at it.

One way this can happen is for the body's immune defense system to put up such a terrific fight that it quickly destroys all the virus in the body—just wipes it out. This means the virus has to hop around and find some other human being to invade, and then another, and then another. By throwing the virus out this way, the immune system prevents it from doing too much damage to anybody, so that everybody who is infected recovers from the infection. But as long as there are plenty of virus particles around, and plenty of other human beings to infect, the virus can at least survive, going from door to door begging, so to speak. This is what happens to most cold viruses, for example. It was also typical of the red measles virus before we had a measles vaccination—new youngsters coming along kept getting measles, but hardly anybody ever died from it.

Another way that a virus can adapt for survival is to change its genetic material or its protein envelope a little bit, from time to time, so that when it comes back to the human being it invaded once before, that person's immune system doesn't recognize it. This kind of genetic change is called a *mutation,* and some viruses that affect human beings mutate quite readily and frequently. The prime examples of this are the so-called influenza viruses that cause the common flu.

Here the biological balance—the peaceful coexistence—is that most people don't die of the flu, but the same person can get it over and over every three or four years because the flu virus keeps changing into something a little different.

There is still another way that some viruses adapt to life with human beings (or vice versa): the viruses find some place to hide in the human body where the immune system can't easily get at them. The trade-off here is that as long as the virus is in hiding it can't be out around the body causing symptoms. It only emerges from hiding once in a while, maybe under special circumstances, to make the person sick. On the other hand, the body never gets rid of the virus, either; it just hangs around forever.

This is exactly what happens with some human herpes viruses. For example, the herpes zoster virus (HZV) attacks just about everyone during childhood, causing chicken pox. The chicken pox victims don't usually die because the body's immune system starts fighting the virus immediately. But as soon as that happens, the HZV runs and hides in clusters of nerve cells around the body where, for reasons we don't understand, the immune system can't get at it. Then, perhaps many years later, HZV can reemerge and cause the painful skin disease known as shingles. The herpes simplex virus that causes genital herpes does much the same thing, but tends to recur more often and gives the victim a lot more trouble. The important point is that once these herpes viruses get into the body, *they never go away. They are lodged somewhere in the body for life.* The hepatitis B virus is different in some ways and similar in others. It is usually destroyed by the immune system after an infection, but not always. In some people the virus somehow becomes impervious to the immune system and persists for years in the bloodstream or liver. These people may seem to have recovered completely but in fact have become *carriers,* and can go on transmitting the live virus to others indefinitely through sexual contact, for example, or by sharing dirty hypodermic needles.

Or a virus can *adapt* itself to its human host—a very sneaky and unpleasant ability. Suppose a particular virus is extremely virulent—it does a great deal of damage to the body and kills many of its victims. But it may not kill *everybody* who is infected, and it may take a long, long time to kill the ones it does kill. Meanwhile, the infected person (who may not even know he or she is sick for a long while) can go right on transmitting the live virus, by sexual contact or other means, to more and more people, so that the virus spreads rapidly in the population. Let's also suppose that this particular virus has the specific action of progressively disabling the body's immune system by slowly destroying the very cells that form the backbone of that immune system, so that the body of the infected person slowly loses its ability to fight back.

Obviously the virus we are describing is very dangerous, and it happens that this description fits the AIDS virus, HIV, perfectly.

A MATTER OF TIMING

At this point it might be fair to ask why this whole complicated business of adaptation, of give and take, between a virus and its human host should take place at all. If we're talking about an all-out war for survival between virus and host, then why isn't it just a matter of kill or be killed?

One possible answer is that such an arrangement would not make much biological sense either for the virus or the host. There are very few, if any, situations in nature in which a life form has developed in such a way that it is forced to destroy itself. As far as science has been able to observe, survival and reproduction are the goals of life, not self-destruction, and this applies to unpleasant entities like viruses as well as to anything else.

Suppose there were a virus that absolutely had to get inside living human cells in order to reproduce and make more viruses, yet by its virulent nature it always destroyed every human being that it ever infected. What would the virus then do when all human beings had been wiped out? Once the virus had destroyed all its hosts, it would have no place to go—it would have destroyed itself, too. And this wouldn't make biological sense. Somehow the virus would have to leave a back door open, an escape hatch, in order to survive. And as we will see, the very virulent HIV virus has found a way to leave the back door open—by way of its long latent period. As one early researcher remarked, "It is a very sneaky virus indeed. . ."

There are two terms we need to know in order to understand the timing of virus behavior in general and HIV behavior in particular. One of the terms is *incubation period,* the other *latent period.* With some viruses these terms amount to the same thing, but with others they don't.

It takes a certain amount of time—minutes, hours, or days—from the time a virus first contacts a susceptible host cell in a human being to the time the virus becomes well enough entrenched in the host to begin causing the damage that leads to disease symptoms. This is the time it takes the virus to invade the first host cells, get its virus DNA attached to the cell's DNA, and get more virus particles replicated and out into the bloodstream to attack more cells. This interval, during which the virus is very active but we see no sign of it, is called the *incubation period.* In some viruses the incubation period may be very short, as little as a few hours, while in others it may be days or even weeks. The chicken pox virus seems to move very fast—you're sick two days after you're exposed—whereas it takes about eighteen days after contact with the measles virus before your fever goes up and the rash appears.

In other viruses, however, there can be a much more prolonged interval between the first infective contact and the first sign of disease symptoms—such a long interval that the virus may appear to be inactive, perhaps even dormant, whether it actually is or not. This kind of prolonged interval, which may stretch on for months or even years, is spoken of as a *latent period.*

Why do certain viruses have long latent periods? One reason can be that it may take a virus a long time after first entry into the body to find the particular host cells it needs to invade. With the rabies virus, for instance, months may pass after an infected animal bite before the victim comes down with the symptoms of rabies which arise from damage and destruction of brain cells. It appears to take the virus a long while to get into the right cells—and doctors have observed in many cases that the closer the bite to the head, the shorter the latent period with this particular virus.

In other cases different factors may explain the long latent period. In a normal, healthy person the immune system usually goes into high gear soon after the initial infective contact with the virus, trying to fight off and destroy the virus. One of the things that happens, as we will see later, is that cells in the immune system begin manufacturing protective *antibodies*, little bundles of protein that circulate in the blood and tend to inactivate a virus whenever they come in contact with it. In the case of some viruses this can develop into a prolonged life-and-death struggle, with the virus fighting to gain and keep a foothold in the host, and the immune system fighting to eradicate it. We can sometimes tell this is happening long before any symptoms begin because these antibodies appear in large numbers in the bloodstream and can be detected by laboratory tests. Since the antibodies don't get into the bloodstream by magic, the fact that they are there clearly tells us that the virus is there also (or at least that it *has* been there). It just hasn't started causing symptoms yet. In some cases this struggle may go on for months or even years before symptoms first appear. And this is exactly what seems to be happening in cases of AIDS.

Yet another reason for a long latent period might be that a given virus just isn't an active reproducer, so an extended period must pass for enough viruses to be replicated to begin causing noticeable damage or destruction. And then, even after such a long latent period, there may be a succession of different or changing symptoms before the final manifestations of the full-blown disease appear. This also appears to be characteristic of AIDS.

A DIFFERENT KIND
OF VIRUS

Let's look at this AIDS virus, HIV, and its cousins HTLV-I and HTLV-II, a little more closely. First of all, these viruses are different from most other viruses in a very fundamental way. All three fall into a special and uncommon class of viruses known as *retroviruses.* Unlike the vast majority of viruses, in which the genetic material is composed of DNA and merely needs to be copied by the host cell in order to make new viruses, the genetic material in retroviruses comes only in the somewhat incomplete form of RNA. In a sense, these viruses are relative cripples. In order to be replicated within the host cell they must grab an additional chunk of the host cell's genetic material—DNA—and add it to their own genetic material in order to become complete enough to force the host cell to make copies of them. These viruses are specially equipped to take this necessary additional step for replication because they contain a special enzyme called *reverse transcriptase* which, in essence, enables these viruses to "write their RNA backwards" to form DNA in the host cells.

The fact is that these retroviruses are exceedingly primitive viruses even as viruses go; they come only halfway equipped. There aren't very many of them known, and all of them characteristically have a very long latent period. One retrovirus you may have heard of, the feline leukemia virus, can cause leukemia in cats—but in some cats it can also cause a disease that

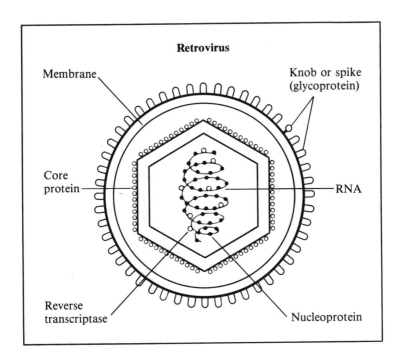

Retrovirus

Membrane

Knob or spike
(glycoprotein)

Core
protein

RNA

Reverse
transcriptase

Nucleoprotein

seems very similar to AIDS in humans. Another such
virus causes a fatal illness called scrapie in sheep. And
among humans, retroviruses are known to cause an
extremely rare, fatal disease known as kuru and/or a
destructive brain disease called Creutzfeld-Jacob syndrome.

For a long time, virus researchers had suspected
that retroviruses might also be involved in the development of certain kinds of human cancers, particularly
leukemias and lymphomas, cancers of the blood and
lymph glands. One theory was that certain of these
very primitive viruses might not only invade a cell and
force its DNA to manufacture more viruses, but in
some cases might also attach its viral genetic material—its RNA—to the cell's DNA in such a way as to

change the genetic nature of the whole cell, so that the cell would subsequently begin dividing and redividing in the wild, uncontrolled manner of cancer cells. In such a case the victim's immune system might suddenly have a large number of sick, deranged cells—cancer cells—to contend with as well as the virus itself.

In the case of HTLV-I and HTLV-II, this seemed to be what was happening. These viruses, attacking lymphocyte-forming cells in the bone marrow, seemed capable of transforming some of those cells into cancer cells. And these transformed cells were not destroyed by the virus invasion. They went right on living and multiplying wildly, resulting in two different forms of blood cell cancer, or leukemia.

We now know that the AIDS virus, HIV, does something a little different, but equally dangerous, in the long run. The main cells it attacks, certain kinds of lymphocytes known as *T-helper cells* or *T4 cells,* do manufacture more virus particles, but are destroyed in the process. This might seem better than having them become cancer cells except for one thing: the T-helper cells that are destroyed normally form one of the vital pillars of the body's immune defense system. At the same time other lymphocytes known as *B-cells,* essential to the production of antibodies against viruses, are also infected and impaired. In addition, still other protective white cells known as *monocytes* or *macrophages* are attacked. These cells seem to serve as reservoirs for the virus and may play a major role in transporting the virus to the brain. Some scientists think these cells may turn out to be even more important than the death of T4 cells in the downward spiral of the disease. In any event, as all these cells are destroyed or impaired in greater and greater numbers,

Mature form

Budding particles

Thus we have a picture of a virulent virus—a new virus on the human scene—that engages in a deadly war against the infected person's immune system. Interestingly enough, HIV doesn't seem to be very hardy or tough, as viruses go. It can't survive very long outside the human body and is easily destroyed by common household disinfectants, including ordinary hand soap. It doesn't even seem to be very good at setting up housekeeping once it gets into the body. There is considerable evidence that the virus may, in many individuals, need to be introduced into the body many times through different or repeated exposures before it can succeed in getting entrenched. Yet in other documented cases a *single contact* with an infected person has been enough to transmit the infection.

Once HIV does get entrenched, the damage it does to the immune system and other organ systems can be profound. To better understand the terrible long-range consequences of this infection, we should review some basic facts about how the immune defense system works, and what kinds of things can happen when it breaks down.

CHAPTER FOUR

THE
SLOW DEATH
OF
IMMUNITY

It is only within the past fifty years or so that medical scientists have come to realize how absolutely vital to healthy human life the body's immune protective system really is, and only within the past thirty years that we have finally begun to understand in detail how that immune system works.

We have known for a long time what happens to the human body when it *doesn't* work. Some few unfortunate people are born without any immune system—the organs and tissues that would normally make up that defense system just aren't there at all, or else fail to function properly because of the individual's hereditary pattern. Typically, these people live short, unhappy lives. They are constantly and repeatedly attacked by infection after infection—infections caused by bacteria, protozoans, rickettsias, viruses, fungi, yeasts, or other parasites—and their bodies have no way to fight back. They develop a variety of different kinds of cancer far earlier and far more frequently than those cancers would appear in normal people because there is no functioning immune system to keep a brand-new, tentative cancerous growth in check or destroy it before it can really start growing.

This condition is called an inborn *combined immune deficiency disease.* Until recently it was only by keeping such people totally isolated from the rest of the world—as in perfectly sterile plastic bubbles—and fighting down infections time after time, that they could be kept alive at all. Recently, researchers have been attempting to install an immune protective system in such people by means of bone marrow grafts or transplants from people with healthy immune systems, and there is reason to hope that such techniques, once fully explored, may prove successful in many cases. Without some breakthrough of this sort, their chances for survival are very poor.

Other people have impaired immune systems because doctors have deliberately made them that way. The person who must have a kidney transplant because his or her natural kidneys have failed is in real jeopardy because the healthy immune system may set to work to reject and destroy the transplanted kidney. To prevent that, doctors will use various hormones and immunosuppressive drugs to slow down the immune system enough that the transplanted kidney can survive and function. This involves a continuing balancing act, suppressing the immune system just enough to prevent rejection of the kidney but not so much that the person begins having all sorts of dangerous infections.

Now, with the appearance of AIDS, we see a new and particularly deadly form of attack upon the body's immune system—an acquired virus agent that causes an immune deficiency so profound and severe that the victim ultimately cannot survive. But how does this attack occur, and how exactly does the immune system become so profoundly deficient?

THE ORGANS OF IMMUNITY

The key to the body's immune protective system is a group of cells known as lymphocytes, which are able to distinguish between those proteins and other chemical substances that naturally belong inside the body because they are part of the individual's biochemical "self" and other proteins and chemical substances that gain entrance into the body from outside it, and are therefore foreign or "not-self" substances. These lymphocytes are programmed by their genetic makeup to be able to recognize and approve the "self" proteins and chemicals they encounter in the body, and leave them alone. But they are also programmed to recognize any foreign or "not-self" substances they encounter, and to trigger a dramatic response whenever they do. These substances don't belong in the body, and must either be neutralized in some way or destroyed. What is more, the lymphocytes are further programmed to "remember" every "not-self" substance they have ever reacted against before and to initiate a very rapid defensive response against that substance any time it might reappear.

How do lymphocytes manage to do all this? These lymphocytes, which are surprisingly long-lived cells inside the body, are originally formed by special lymphocyte-making *precursor cells* that reside in the soft, spongy red bone marrow found in the ends of the long bones of the arms and legs, in the bones of the pelvis, or in the interior of the rib bones, for example. But several different kinds of lymphocytes eventually develop from these precursor cells.

One kind of lymphocyte is released into the bloodstream and goes to work immediately searching out "not-self" substances. These lymphocytes—known as *B-cells* because they come directly from the bone marrow—circulate with the blood and travel out through the thin walls of tiny capillaries into all the tissues and organs in the body, acting like wandering military patrolmen constantly on the lookout for foreign substances. In some areas of the body—in the neck, under the arms, in the groin, or in the abdomen, for instance—these B-lymphocytes congregate and lodge in small, spongy meshworks of fibrous tissue to form glandlike structures called *lymph glands.* When a wandering lymphocyte encounters a foreign sub-stance—the protein envelope of an invading virus, for example, or one of the poisons exuded by some invading bacteria—it takes a sort of biochemical measurement of the shape of the foreign protein and then carries it back to the lymph glands.

Here special variants of the B-cell known as *plasma cells* begin manufacturing natural protein substances called *antibodies.* These antibodies are specifically designed to the exact measurement of the foreign protein and are built in such a way that when that specific antibody encounters that protein molecule it will lock onto it and immobilize it, much as a defensive right guard on a football team will block or immobilize an opposing player who is going after his quarterback. At the same time, the antibody helps stimulate the activity of other natural protein substances in the circulating blood, known as *complement molecules,* to rally around and help destroy the foreign invader.

Meanwhile other white blood cells in the body join the battle. These are not lymphocytes at all but larger cells called *monocytes.* Sometimes these cells are also called *macrophages*—literally, "big eaters"—because their job is to wander through the body, gather at the site of an infection, and engulf and digest the bacteria or viruses that have been immobilized by the antibodies or destroyed by complement molecules.

THE INDISPENSABLE T-CELLS

The B-cells can't manage this whole job of identification and antibody manufacture all by themselves, however. They need something to help regulate them—to tell them how fast to make antibodies, how many to make, and when to stop making them. There are times, for example, when the B-cells have to be called swiftly into action to make lots and lots of antibodies fast in the face of an overwhelming threat such as a virus invasion. At other times, after the danger is over, they tend to keep right on manufacturing antibodies at full speed and need some influence to slow them down or suppress this activity.

The immune system manages this delicate balancing act through the action of two other groups of lymphocytes that are quite different from the B-cells. These two groups of cells, after being formed in the bone marrow, are acted upon by hormonelike substances manufactured in the thymus gland (a soft, spongy organ that lies in the front of the chest just below the throat) and are therefore called T-lympho-cytes or T-cells. One of these groups of T-cells acts to *speed up* antibody production by the B-cells. Cells in this group are spoken of as *T-helper cells.* The other group takes on the opposite function: to slow down or *suppress* antibody production when the threat is over and more antibodies aren't needed. Cells in this second group are called *T-suppressor cells.* Because of special details of their biochemical structure, immunologists sometimes speak of the T-helper lymphocytes as "T4 cells" and T-suppressor cells as "T8 cells."

In a normal, healthy individual the T-helper cells and T-suppressor cells are usually found in the bloodstream in a fairly fixed ratio of about two T-helper cells for each T-suppressor cell. Thus, if a cubic milliliter of a person's blood contains eight hundred T-helper cells, you would expect to find about four hundred T-suppressor cells in the same volume of blood, a ratio of 2 to 1. This ratio is important; one of the ways that laboratory tests can help determine when something bad is going on with a person's immune system—often long before any symptoms or signs appear—is to detect a change in that 2 to 1 ratio between T-helper cells and T-suppressor cells in the person's blood. For example, if something is destroying T-helper cells so fast that their numbers are reduced to only four hundred per cubic milliliter of blood, while the T-suppressor cells remain at four hundred, the ratio of T-helper cells to T-suppressor cells is changed from 2 to 1 to 1 to 1, and the doctor suspects that something unusual is going on. If that ratio drops even further, say to 0.8 to 1, the doctor *knows* the patient's cellular immune system has become defective or deficient, and that that patient is in deep trouble even if there are no symptoms or other clues at all.

Finally, there is a third group of T-lymphocytes, also acted upon by thymus gland hormones so that they, too, are T-cells, but different from both the T-helper cells and the T-suppressor cells. These lymphocytes are known as *natural killer cells* or NK cells. Their job is to go to the place where a dangerous foreign invader has been found (a newly formed cancer cell, for example). The killer cell then makes direct contact with the dangerous cell and destroys it. Some fascinating microphotography movies were made some years ago by Dr. Michael Beane at the Virginia Mason Research Center in Seattle, showing natural killer cells in action. The NK cells were put into a culture where malignant cells were growing. Through the microscope it is actually possible to see these killer cells encounter a cancer cell, press against it, stick to it, surround it, until suddenly, before your eyes, the cancer cell disintegrates!

What we have been describing, essentially, represents two parts of the immune defensive system. One part, including the circulating antibodies and complement molecules in the bloodstream, is called the *humoral* immune system (because blood was one of the four "humors" described by ancient physicians). The other part, involving the T-helper and T-suppressor cells and the NK cells, is the *cellular* immune system. Of course, these two parts of the system work together. But researchers have noticed an interesting thing. The humoral immune system seems to be targeted primarily against bacterial infections, bacterial poisons, and many common virus infections. The cellular immune system seems to be more concerned with protecting the body against yeast and fungus infections, protozoan infections, certain special virus infections, and certain kinds of cancers. We will come back to this distinction later, because it seems to have a particular application to AIDS.

ENTER HIV

What we have just been discussing is a very brief and simplified outline of the way some parts of an extremely complex organ system—the body's immune system—work to fight off a variety of foreign invaders and, in some cases, to protect against the early emergence of certain kinds of cancers. Obviously this outline is not the whole picture. There are immunologists, virologists, and other researchers who have spent their lives trying to fully understand and sort out the many intricacies of how the immune system works in health and disease, and the picture is still not complete by any means. But this outline at least gives us some of the basic facts and ideas we need in order to understand what the AIDS virus, HIV, does to the immune system and what the long-term results of this damage can be.

At some point, a person who has never before had contact with HIV comes in contact with it. From what we know now, this infecting contact has to occur from contact with the blood or body fluids of someone who is already infected and has the live virus present in his or her bloodstream and tissues. In the majority of cases this means a sexual contact and, according to clues that researchers have picked up about the pattern of the disease, probably in most cases a frequent, recur-

fewer sexual contacts—as if the virus needed frequent and repeated chances to break down a person's resistance before effective infection can take place. Maybe the immune system keeps slapping down this virus very early after contact unless it is overwhelmed by continuous virus contacts. This seems to apply to modes of infection other than sexual contact, too. The frequent and regular illicit intravenous drug user is more likely to become infected than the person who participates only rarely, and the hemophilic who must have repeated transfusions of blood products is more vulnerable to infection than the person who has to have just one unit of blood given during an operation. But in all such cases, of course, plain common sense dictates that the more opportunities for contact with the virus a person has, the more likely an infecting contact will occur.

Once the HIV virus gains entry into the body, it makes its way through the bloodstream to the places where lymphocytes are most likely to be found: the bone marrow, the lymph glands, or the bloodstream itself. Having found its preferred tissue—the lymphocytes—the virus must then break into individual cells. Some incubation period between the initial contact with the virus and its activity inside the lymphocytes must occur, but nobody knows how long it may be. Possibly a person must carry the virus in the bloodstream for a prolonged interval before it finally gains entry into vulnerable lymph cells. Maybe the virus gets into the lymph cells almost immediately, but then just sits there for a long time before it does anything. In other words, maybe it has a prolonged dormant or latent period. There have been cases in which the time of initial contact with the virus was known exactly, but actual symptoms of physical illness didn't begin to appear for as long as two, three, or four years or longer. In other cases, patients have been known to have the virus in the bloodstream but had not yet formed antibodies against the virus, suggesting that it had not yet been detected by the immune system. As we will see later, this is a major problem when we count on HIV antibody tests to determine whether a person is or is not infected. As much as six months or even a year may elapse after a person has been infected before that person *sero-converts,* or develops detectable antibodies in his or her blood stream. Yet during that interval, when the person still tests antibody-negative, he or she may already be able to transmit the virus to uninfected people.

A SILENT AND SYMPTOMLESS INFECTION

Whatever the incubation period or the latent period may be, sooner or later the virus finds its way into lymphocytes and commandeers them to start producing more viruses. This leads to two end results: the destruction of the lymphocytes after the new viruses have been made, and the appearance of the new viruses in the bloodstream on their way to seek out other lymphocytes. HIV seems to seek out one kind of lymphocyte in particular—the T-helper lymphocytes—and as those cells are selectively invaded and destroyed, the total number of T-helper cells in the body slowly begins to decline. At the same time, the white blood cells called macrophages seem to act as protective reservoirs for the virus in the body, and may help the virus find its way through natural barriers into brain cells as well.

Meanwhile, the virus in the bloodstream or active in the T-helper lymphocytes is soon discovered by the wandering B-lymphocytes. Its protein coating is identified as "not-self" and that message is carried back to the plasma cells, which begin churning out specific antibodies against the virus and releasing them into the bloodstream. You'll notice that up to this point, things are working much the same as they would with any virus infection. Antibodies appear in the victim's bloodstream. Laboratory tests can be done to identify these antibodies, thus demonstrating that the virus is indeed inside the body even though no symptoms of illness have appeared. In fact, in many cases at this point, the virus itself could actually be grown in a laboratory culture from a sample of the patient's blood, semen, or other body fluids.

You might think that this would be the ideal way to find out for sure if a person were infected with HIV or not. Unfortunately, actually identifying the virus itself is an extremely complicated, time-consuming, and costly procedure that involves incubating the blood sample that may contain the virus with a collection of healthy lymphocytes obtained from a known uninfected source, then adding biological substances to promote or accelerate the viruses' replication in the healthy lymphocytes, and so forth. While this procedure is possible and has been successfully performed, there are relatively few virology laboratories in the country equipped to do it, and the time, labor, and costly or rare biochemical agents consumed make the procedure prohibitively expensive except for very special research purposes. It just isn't practical for any kind of widespread screening test. The tests available to detect the antibodies, however, are relatively easy and inexpensive and can be done by a wide variety of laboratories. Thus it's far more practical to try to pin down the presence of the virus by "finding its footprints"—detecting the antibodies formed against it in a person's body—rather than trying to catch the virus itself.

But if the chain of events following an HIV invasion has seemed much the same as with any virus invasion so far, at this point things begin to happen that definitely do not happen in a case of, say, measles or chicken pox. As the virus attacks, commandeers, and destroys its T-helper lymphocyte host cells, a few at a time, more and more viruses are poured out into the bloodstream to attack, commandeer, and destroy more and more T-helper lymphocytes. But because it is primarily the T-helper cells that the virus is attacking and destroying, the body's immune defenses slowly but surely begin to weaken. Losing those T-helper cells means that the B-lymphocytes' job of producing antibodies against the virus is hampered, since it is the T-helper cells that speed up that process during an emergency, and they are the cells that are being destroyed. In addition, there is evidence that the AIDS virus may also directly impair the functions of the B-lymphocytes as well. As the infection progresses, the B-cells not only slowly lose their ability to make antibodies; they also seem to lose their ability to "remember" the foreign protein substance or antigen that they're making the antibodies against. And the monocytes that congregate at the infection site to devour viruses seem to be impaired in their function as well.

The overall effect, over a prolonged period of time, is that of a silent, symptomless, but ever-growing infection in which the attacking virus increases in number and strength in the body, the T-helper cells decrease steadily in number, the B-lymphocytes and monocytes are progressively impaired in doing their work, and the victim's immune protective system begins to fall apart bit by bit.

CHAPTER FIVE

THE SIGNS AND SYMPTOMS OF AIDS

While the slow death of immunity progresses in an AIDS-infected person, a number of different things can begin to happen. As time passes, the HIV infection moves from a silent, symptom-free period (sometimes long, sometimes short) to a point where recognizable signs and symptoms begin to appear. These signs and symptoms can be so variable, so different from one person to another, that to understand them we need to identify different patterns of symptoms—different possible scenarios, so to speak—by number.

A BEWILDERING PATTERN OF ILLNESS

1) At some point after infection with the virus—perhaps as little as a month or as long as a year after the first infective contact—*antibodies* against HIV will begin to appear in the person's bloodstream. These are the special proteins manufactured by the person's

immune system in an attempt to fight off the HIV invasion. The appearance of these antibodies, detected by special blood tests, is the *first clear-cut sign that that person has indeed been infected by HIV.*

What does this mean? Because the antibodies are there, it means that the *virus* is there too—the antibodies didn't get there by magic. What's more, AIDS experts today believe that HIV infection is for life; once the virus is in the body, the person never gets rid of it. It also means the virus is probably present not only in the person's blood but in other body fluids as well—in the semen, in vaginal secretions, in saliva, and so forth. It is just most highly concentrated in the blood and semen. And that means that the person has become *infective*—that is, *he or she can now transmit the virus to other people,* whether any symptoms have appeared or not.

You might think, from this, that a blood test for AIDS antibodies would tell *definitely and for certain* whether a person was infected by HIV or not. But it's not that simple. For one thing, the antibody tests are not 100 percent accurate. (We'll have more to say about those tests later.) Even more important is the lag between the time of infection and the first appearance of antibodies—anywhere from a month to a year. If the antibody tests are definitely positive, it means the person is infected. But if the tests are negative, that person *may nevertheless be infected—and infective*—anyway and the antibodies just haven't appeared in the blood stream yet. *This is a very important point that we'll come back to when we talk about prevention of AIDS.*

2) The appearance of antibodies is the first measurable sign of infection, but they do not in themselves

indicate any *active illness.* At some point later—maybe a year after the initial infection, maybe two or three years later, maybe even seven or eight years later—active illness may begin to show up in a series of vague, nonspecific, but very troublesome symptoms. In some cases daily fevers begin to occur, rising to as much as 104°F (40°C) each day and then breaking. Along with these fevers, some persons may have episodes of profuse sweating during the night. These episodes may go on day after day or night after night. In addition, some individuals may begin having frequent, sometimes debilitating, bouts of diarrhea on a daily basis, often associated with abdominal cramps, sometimes with nausea and vomiting. Any or all of these symptoms may be accompanied by steady, unexplained weight loss, sometimes with a loss of appetite as well. (Among AIDS patients in Africa weight loss is so common and pronounced that AIDS is sometimes called "the wasting illness" or "the slim disease.") In some individuals these various symptoms, once started, may persist for weeks and months. In others they come and go quite erratically. We might speak of the people with these sorts of symptoms as falling into "Group A."

3) Other individuals begin showing evidence of their infection in a different way. For some, the first apparent sign of trouble comes in the form of swollen lymph glands in the throat, under the arms, or in the groin—swelling that doesn't have any apparent explanation. Some people with this kind of *lymphadenopathy* may have some of the other symptoms, too—fevers and night sweats, for example—and many also begin noticing unexplained weight loss, but the lymphadenopathy seems to be the *primary* signal that something

is wrong. And like the other symptoms, this lymphade-nopathy (which may become quite marked) seems to persist or even get worse over a period of weeks, months, or longer. We might call these people members of "Group B."

4) While the symptoms we have mentioned in people in Group A or Group B are often extremely troublesome, at least they are symptoms that people can live with; unpleasant as they are, there doesn't seem to be anything particularly deadly or dangerous about them. However, for most people in Group A or Group B, something new and decidedly dangerous will appear within another time period ranging from weeks or months to a year or two. Sooner or later they suddenly and unexpectedly come down with one or another of a group of so-called "opportunistic infections."

One such infection frequently encountered is an extremely severe case of candidiasis, or thrush, involving the mouth, throat, or esophagus, caused by infection with a yeast called *Candida albicans*. Ordinarily this infection is seen only in mild form in otherwise normal babies as a white, patchy growth inside the cheeks or on the gums or the tongue. But in the case of AIDS-infected people the thrush can become so severe and extensive that eating and swallowing become extremely painful and difficult, if not impossible.

Such an infection is called "opportunistic" for an obvious reason. In a normal person with a normal immune system, such a *Candida* infection would never be able to gain a foothold at all, because the body's immune system would fight it down and destroy it before it ever had a chance to become entrenched. The only times that such an infection might appear in an adult with a normal immune system would be in people who had uncontrolled diabetes and lived in a very warm climate where a lot of perspiration was common. In such cases the infection might appear as a skin inflammation on the chest or in such warm, damp areas as the underarms. More rarely, the infection might appear in the bowel of a normal person as a mild "overgrowth" when the normal bowel bacteria have been wiped out by heavy doses of antibiotics. But when a person's immune system is *not* working properly, the *Candida albicans* yeast has a perfect opportunity to move in like an invading army because the person's body no longer has any way to fight it off.

Some of the other opportunistic infections that AIDS-infected patients may fall heir to are:

Pneumocystis carinii pneumonia. We know that the *Pneumocystis carinii* protozoan organism is all around us in the environment. In fact, there is reason to suspect that some 50 to 75 percent of all people actually have *Pneumocystis* infections during early childhood. Normally, researchers think, this protozoan infection is beaten back by the immune system but not totally eradicated—it simply goes dormant in the body and then normally remains dormant for the rest of the individual's life. Healthy people practically never have a recurrence of this infection. But with an important part of the immune system knocked out by HIV infection, the *Pneumocystis* can recur with a vengeance in the form of a deadly, fast-moving pneumonia.

Cryptococcus infection. The organism known as *Cryptococcus neoformans* is a yeastlike fungus that does occasionally attack normal people, although not very often. In such people it often forms *abcesses* (localized pockets of infection) in the lung or in the brain. But in patients with AIDS it appears much more frequently in a more wide-spread form that is often associated with meningitis.

Toxoplasma gondii infection. In some hospitals treating AIDS patients, infection with a protozoan organism known as *Toxoplasma gondii* is very common and often appears in the form of an abcess in the brain. Like *Pneumocystis,* it may be that this protozoan is acquired by many people early in life, stopped by the immune system before it can do any harm, and then becomes reactivated when the immune defenses fall apart because of an AIDS virus infection.

Herpes simplex infections, oral or genital, or Cytomegalovirus infections. These infections are common enough among male homosexuals without having anything to do with AIDS, but in the presence of AIDS they can appear in extreme, even fatal, forms as opportunistic infections that can simply overwhelm the immune-deficient individual.

5) There is still another kind of symptom, quite different from opportunistic infections, that can herald the onset of AIDS. It is now known that the HIV virus is not only *lymphotropic* (seeking out lymph cells) but also *neurotropic* (seeking out brain cells) as well. Quite aside from destroying the immune system by killing T-helper cells, with all the attendant immune-deficiency symptoms we have been talking about, HIV can also destroy brain cells.

The symptoms that can result from this destruction have nothing to do with immunity, but they can have a great deal to do with how the person behaves and how his or her brain functions. Some of these symptoms can be very subtle—a slight deterioration in vision or hearing, for example, or a slight deficit in the memory function or judgment. Doctors hear relatives and friends of such a person saying, "It's hard to put your finger on it, but Jack has changed. He doesn't seem quite the same person anymore." Others have marked, progressive memory lapses, or trouble working their muscles, or gross mental disturbances that doctors call "dementia." Many AIDS researchers now believe there are large numbers of HIV-infected persons who may not show any particular immune system defects or other symptoms of full-blown AIDS but do show subtle or marked brain damage from the virus—and this, too, is diagnostic of AIDS.

Why don't people with AIDS seem to get more ordinary bacterial infections, such as pneumococcus pneumonia or strep throat, if their immune systems are so depressed? At the time this book is written, nobody can answer that question for sure. It may have to do with which part of the immune system is depressed the most at first. We know it is the cellular immune system—which gives the most protection against yeast, fungal, and protozoan infections, as well as certain kinds of cancer—that seems to deteriorate first. The humoral immune system—the antibodies and complement molecules that help fight off ordinary bacterial infections—may remain intact longer, so that it is the exotic opportunistic infections that dig in first. But recently researchers have noticed a sharp increase in one very deadly "ordinary" bacterial infection—tuberculosis—among AIDS-infected patients. Not only does the AIDS immune deficiency seem to allow previous, dormant TB infections to recur more easily, it seems to make the victims more vulnerable to new TB infections as well. And a number of bizarre tuberculosis-like infections caused by bacterial cousins of the tuberculosis bacillus are also frequently reported in AIDS patients—infections previously rarely seen at all!

(6) Finally, a number of AIDS-infected people begin developing certain forms of cancer that were previously quite rare, presumably because the normal immune system destroyed these cancers early in their development, before they got well-established. The most common of these cancers is the Kaposi's sarcoma we mentioned earlier, essentially a cancer of the blood vessels in and just beneath the skin. Another kind of cancer that appears with uncommon frequency is a cancer of the lymph glands known as *lymphoma.*

All these opportunistic infections and cancers have one further unpleasant characteristic. In the absence of a good, fully functioning immune system, these afflictions are extremely difficult to treat. There are a few drugs that can help fight candidiasis or *Pneumocystis carinii* pneumonia, but treatment tends to be a long, hard struggle, and the infections tend to recur very quickly just as soon as an apparently successful course of treatment is terminated. Kaposi's sarcoma can also be effectively treated—or at least partially suppressed or temporarily slowed down with radiation treatment or chemotherapy—but it also tends to recur. Thus, these people seem to go into repeated episodes of infection or repeated recurrences of their cancers. They are constantly in and out of hospitals and seem no sooner to get one problem cleared up than another one appears. And ultimately, one by one, these sufferers reach a point where treatment just doesn't work anymore and they finally die.

"AIDS-RELATED COMPLEX" AND "FULL-BLOWN AIDS"

It was hardly any wonder that this kind of illness, which could manifest itself in so many different forms, seemed extremely mysterious or confusing when it first appeared. To add to the confusion, there was the fact that some people who began developing symptoms in Group A or Group B never did go on to develop the deadly succession of opportunistic infections we have described, or did so only years later. Perhaps only 20 percent (one out of five) of those in Group A or Group B soon went on to develop what came to be known as "full-blown AIDS," that is, actually began to develop the opportunistic infections or cancers that would ultimately kill them.

Later, when the AIDS virus or HIV was finally identified, and when tests were developed to check a person's blood serum for antibodies and thus determine if the person was indeed infected or not, it was found that virtually all the people in Group A or Group B were just as thoroughly infected as those who progressed to develop full-blown AIDS. But early in the epidemic, if you were trying to guess what was going to happen to a given patient, it seemed very important to know whether a sick person fell into Groups A or B or into the group with full-blown AIDS. In an attempt to classify people into the different groups, doctors and public health officials during the early 1980s began to speak of people in Group A, with their fevers and night sweats and diarrhea and weight loss, as having a condition called *AIDS-Related Complex* or *ARC*. Those in Group B were described as having *Lymphadenopathy Syndrome* or *LAS.* Only those who went on to develop potentially fatal opportunistic infections or Kaposi's sarcoma were classified as having "full-blown AIDS." Nobody knew what was going to happen, eventually, to the ARC or LAS patients. It appeared, at the time, that only those with full-blown AIDS were certain to die of the disease. Needless to say, all this became very confusing to doctors and researchers who were trying to keep track of a deadly, complicated, and rapidly spreading disease. *Exactly who had AIDS and who didn't?*

THE FIRST GUIDELINES

To help clear the air, back in 1982 or 1983, the U.S. Public Health Service Centers for Disease Control (CDC) for the first time set up some specific *diagnostic guidelines,* or criteria, in order to classify people with AIDS infections. In order to monitor new cases of AIDS nationwide and tell how the disease was spreading, the CDC decided, it was first necessary for everybody to agree on exactly what AIDS was and what it wasn't, according to some clear-cut rules. That way nobody would be diagnosed as having AIDS just because he or she had some peculiar symptoms, and people who did have real, full-blown AIDS could be distinguished from others who had some AIDS-like symptoms but might never actually develop the full-blown disease.

First of all, the CDC specified that the term "AIDS" should refer only to a person who had already developed at least one life-threatening condition—either a severe opportunistic infection or a cancer—of the sort that occurs because of a breakdown of cellular immunity when that person has no other reason for such a breakdown in immunity except infection with the AIDS virus. We have already listed above the major opportunistic infections that came under this umbrella. The immune-deficiency-type cancers that qualify under this surveillance definition were Kaposi's sarcoma in patients younger than sixty years of age (older patients were excluded because they might be among the few people who get Kaposi's sarcoma without AIDS) and lymphomas—lymph gland cancers—that involved lymph tissue in the brain or spinal cord.

This, then, became the first established official definition of what AIDS was. It followed, of course, that anyone who did not have one of these life-threatening conditions should *not* be diagnosed as having AIDS.

But what about those people who developed early AIDS-like symptoms—the people who fell into Group A or Group B—but had never had a life-threatening opportunistic infection or cancer of the sort described in the CDC definition of AIDS? The CDC decided, for purposes of surveillance and study, to put these people into a single illness category under the name of AIDS-Related Complex or ARC. A person was defined as having ARC if some laboratory abnormality indicated that something was wrong with his or her immune system—a reduced number of T-helper cells, for instance, or a ratio of T-helper cells to T-suppressor cells below 1 to 1, or a failure to react normally to allergic skin tests—and who also had at least two of the following symptoms:

- fever greater than 100°F (38°C) for a period of three months or longer,

- weight loss greater than 10 percent or a total loss of 15 or more pounds (7 or more kg),
- lymphadenopathy present for three months or longer,
- diarrhea,
- fatigue,
- night sweats.

In the case of young children, especially babies under six months of age suspected of having AIDS, the CDC added some additional restrictions. First, the doctor suspecting the diagnosis in such a child had to be certain the child did not have some hereditary immune deficiency disease and was not, for any reason, receiving medicine that might suppress the immune system, or have a cancer that was in itself causing immune suppression. The physician had also to be certain that the child did not have one of the opportunistic infections, such as herpes simplex infection or cytomegalovirus infection, that might have been passed to him or her across the mother's placenta.

NEW KNOWLEDGE, NEW GUIDELINES

Those first diagnostic guidelines were immensely helpful in pinpointing what this new and mysterious disease called AIDS was and what it was not, as the disease was understood at the time. For the first time public health authorities, with the help of doctors and researchers all over the country, were able to begin accurate, ongoing surveys of where the disease was appearing, where it was spreading, and how rapidly. But as more was learned about the disease, those guidelines soon proved inadequate. For one thing, they were set up before the AIDS virus had even been discovered or shown to be the cause of AIDS. They were set up long before tests for AIDS virus antibodies had been introduced—a powerful diagnostic tool. And they were set up before it was clearly realized that the AIDS virus could attack the brain as well as the lymphocytes, so that many people with full-blown AIDS might develop mental disturbances and dementia as the first and only early symptom of their disease. This all meant, among other things, that the old guidelines were missing lots of cases, and the ongoing surveys were underestimating the true magnitude of the epidemic.

In August 1987 the CDC published revised and updated guidelines for diagnosis of AIDS. These new guidelines recognized the importance of HIV antibodies in a person's blood as evidence of actual infection with the virus. They broadened the list of "indicator" opportunistic infections and cancers recognized as associated with full-blown AIDS. They formally recognized *HIV brain damage,* ranging from minor memory disturbances all the way to dementia, as a valid diagnostic sign. And they recognized the so-called *HIV wasting syndrome* ("slim disease"), with its diarrhea, weight loss, chronic weakness and persistent fever, as a part of ARC or AIDS-Related Complex. In practical terms the new guidelines recognized ARC as a sort of *prodromal* or developing stage of full-blown AIDS with its opportunistic infections, cancers, or symptomatic brain damage.

THE LONG-TERM PICTURE

Today surveillance of this spreading epidemic continues with increasing urgency as more and more is learned about AIDS. It has become increasingly clear that the outlook for people with full-blown AIDS, diagnosed according to both the old and new CDC guidelines, is gloomy indeed. According to a report from the Centers for Disease Control released in January 1989, a total of over 84,000 patients with full-blown AIDS had been reported in the United States alone since June of 1981. Of these patients, over 47,000 had died. (Just a year earlier the numbers had been 50,000 total patients and 28,000 deaths.) Beginning in 1988, 400 new cases of AIDS were appearing each *week,* and the CDC estimated that there would be 250,000 AIDS cases reported by 1991. Perhaps even more significantly, a high percentage of all of the patients who had been diagnosed before July 1984 had died. The earliest-discovered patients are all gone now. And although it cannot yet be scientifically proven, most doctors who have worked with AIDS patients now believe that once full-blown AIDS has developed, the disease is universally fatal. Some patients may live only a few weeks or months and then die during the first or second attack of an opportunistic infection. Some may respond to treatment better than others and live for two or three years, perhaps even four, but few will survive much longer than that—as things stand today. Unless there is some major scientific breakthrough, some really effective treatment discovered, virtually all those patients will ultimately die of the disease.

But what about those individuals whose positive HIV antibody tests indicate that they have been infected and are thus under attack by the AIDS virus, but have not yet developed the opportunistic infections or cancers or other signs and symptoms that mark the turning point into full-blown AIDS? With the beginning of antibody testing in late 1984, many of these people have been identified. For them, as a group, the picture is certainly brighter than for people who have the full-blown disease, but nobody yet knows just how much brighter. We know that a certain number of these people will eventually develop full-blown AIDS, but we don't know which ones, or how many, or when. Some infected but symptom-free people may begin developing symptoms within a few months. Others may remain symptom-free for years and then suddenly become ill. In December 1987, the CDC reported that the mean interval between the initial infection with HIV and the onset of symptomatic AIDS exceeds seven years.* Current surveillance data indicates that somewhere between 20 and 35 percent of those HIV-positive people will eventually go on to develop full-blown AIDS sooner or later. But some AIDS experts suspect that almost *all* of them will, eventually. Only time and dogged surveillance can tell. This maddeningly indefinite time-lag between time of infection and onset of illness is one of the most frustrating things about AIDS. If you are exposed to the measles virus, you either break out with a rash within 18 days or you don't get the disease at all, and that's that. But HIV is a different virus. Why do some infected people become ill quickly while others encounter no problems for years? At this point, nobody knows for sure. One theory is that a certain degree of immune system impairment will always happen at some point following HIV infection, to represent a first stage in the

*Centers for Disease Control. *Morbidity and Mortality Weekly Report,* Vol. 36, No. 49. December 18, 1987.

natural history of the disease. A certain number of T-helper cells and B-cells will be destroyed or impaired, for example. But this initial damage may not be enough to cause identifiable immune deficiency symptoms; maybe the person's immune system can still fight back effectively enough to prevent that, even though some damage has been done by the virus.

According to this theory, for a high percentage of infected people—perhaps 70 or 80 percent—that first stage may be as far as the disease goes for a long while, maybe for years, and that stage of the disease is survivable. According to this theory, then, only some 20 to 35 percent of infected people sooner or later progress to a second, lethal stage of the disease. These are the ones who develop full-blown AIDS and ultimately die from it. Possibly one reason that some patients develop full-blown AIDS while the others don't is due, in part, to the presence of some other as-yet-unidentified *co-factors* that make them more vulnerable—individual genetic makeup, factors in the environment, nutritional factors, drug actions, or other variables of this sort. Of course, all of this is massively frustrating to all concerned. Scientists like neatness and tidiness above all else; it is hard for them to accept the apparently pointless randomness with which HIV seems to behave in infected persons. They would love to find some reasonable explanation that would allow them to predict who was going to become symptomatic when, and who wasn't, and such an explanation would certainly clear the air a great deal for a great many worried and frightened infected people—but so far no such explanation is yet on the horizon.

It is certainly clear today that for every person in the United States with full-blown AIDS, there are a large number who are infected and harbor the virus but have not yet become sick. Indeed, analyzing the surveillance data they already have, the CDC now estimates that between 1,000,000 and 1,500,000 people in the United States alone are already infected as of early 1988—and some critics contend that those estimates are far too small, that they really should be doubled.*

If these figures are anywhere near true, then in the course of just eight years there has been a wildfire spread of HIV infection among some population groups in this country. Nor can we any longer imagine that this plague is in any way confined exclusively to a few small special "risk groups" such as male homosexuals or intravenous drug users in America. It is spreading in other groups as well, and it is spreading worldwide. At the first international "AIDS Summit" that convened in London in January 1988, attended by 146 national public health officials from all over the world, it was estimated that between 5 and 9 million people were already infected worldwide, that there will be 1,000,000 cases of symptomatic AIDS throughout the world by 1991, and in places such as Europe and central Africa the spread of the disease is predominately among heterosexuals.

THE TIME FACTOR

One major problem in making sense of all this is the fact that there just hasn't been enough time since AIDS made its first appearance for anyone to know for

---

*Centers for Disease Control. *Morbidity and Mortality Weekly Report*, Vol. 36, No. 49. December 18, 1987.

sure what may ultimately happen to that other 70 to 80 percent of patients known to be infected with the HIV virus but not yet showing any signs or symptoms of AIDS. After all, the disease has only been identified for about eight years. Obviously, the best possible scenario for these HIV-infected patients who have escaped early progression to full-blown AIDS would be that after a few more years without any evidence of further change, they may be home free and never will progress to the full-blown disease. Nobody who has studied this disease believes that is going to happen. The worst possible scenario would be that sooner or later, maybe within ten or fifteen or even twenty years, *all* of these people will progress to full-blown AIDS. Some AIDS experts believe that is *exactly* what is going to happen. But at this point, nobody knows, and there is absolutely no way to tell but to wait and see.

Certainly contracting an HIV infection is an extremely dangerous thing to have happen. For many people, it will be a fatal thing to have happen. It is not hard to understand how a widespread fear of the disease exists in the minds of the general public, and it is easy to understand how this fear has been translated into a lot of false ideas and irrational attitudes among people. These fears and falsehoods tend to become more acute and destructive as it becomes increasingly clear that large numbers of people—not just a few— may already have been infected, or may be vulnerable to infection and as it becomes clear that the pattern of spread may be changing in an ominous way.

At first AIDS appeared to be confined to a few small risk groups—male homosexuals and intravenous drug users who were engaged in what much of the rest of the world regarded as aberrant patterns of sexual behavior or life-style—plus a few people trapped into the disease because they were either hemophilics who had to use transfusion blood products, or else were children born to infected mothers. These are still the main risk groups, but it is now becoming clear that the spread of AIDS is no longer confined to these groups exclusively. It is now known that many female prostitutes are infected with the AIDS virus, largely due to intravenous drug needle exposure, and are thus capable of transmitting it to their male clients through sexual contact. It is also known that in some parts of the world—in central Africa, in certain Caribbean islands including Haiti, and in parts of Europe—the disease is primarily transmitted by means of male-female heterosexual contact. And indeed, it seems likely that the spread of the disease in our own country may begin more and more to involve ordinary people, married or not, who are sexually active in more or less ordinary ways—which means a great many potential victims indeed.

In view of this, it is extremely important for us to consider in more detail what is actually true about AIDS, as far as we know today, and what probably isn't true. Only in this way can we see what each of us needs to know and do in order to protect ourselves from the infection.

CHAPTER SIX

WHAT WE KNOW ABOUT HIV INFECTIONS

If there is a bright side to the AIDS picture, it is what we know about the way the infection is—and is *not*—transmitted.

We know, for example, that certain people are in terrible and continuing danger of contracting the HIV infection, and are in danger of transmitting it to others once they themselves are infected, because of their particular sexual practices or life-styles. But it's encouraging to know that far more people—perhaps *most* people—run a far smaller, more controllable risk of contracting the infection, while others run virtually no risk at all, at least at the present time. We know there are several clear-cut ways the infection can be spread from an infected person to a noninfected person—but it is cheering to know that there are also a number of ways that the infection is not ordinarily spread.

Certainly it is wise to worry about possibly contracting this virus infection by the routes that we *know* contribute to its spread. But it doesn't make sense to worry about contracting the disease by routes through which it doesn't seem to spread at all. HIV is not spread by magic, nor in some vague, mysterious, frightening way that nobody understands. Therefore it is very important for us to know who is the most vulnerable to contracting the infection and who is not—and *why*.

THE "HIGHEST RISK" GROUPS

It has been clearly established that a person infected with the AIDS virus will, at one time or another, have live, infective virus in a variety of his or her body fluids. Maybe the virus isn't present in all these fluids constantly, maybe only intermittently—nobody knows for sure—but it may be there at any time.

We know, for example, that the virus is often present in the *blood* of the infected person. We know that it is characteristically present in the *semen* of an infected man, and has been detected in smaller amounts in the *vaginal secretions* of infected women. In a very few instances the live virus has been found in the saliva of an infected person. What about tears, sweat, sputum, or nasal secretions? Theoretically, the virus can be present in such body fluids or secretions, AIDS researchers admit, but the fact is that it has practically never been found in them, possibly because it is present in such small amounts (if at all) that it can't be detected. The important point is that the virus is usually present in far greater numbers in the blood or semen—the most frequently identified contact fluids— and only in very small numbers, if at all, in other body fluids. This means that blood and semen are the two most dangerous major vehicles for HIV transmission, with vaginal secretions a likely third.

Knowing this, we can see certain groups of people who are at exceptionally high risk of contracting the infection, and why they are at such high risk. Obviously, persons who engage in promiscuous sexual activity are at much higher risk of becoming infected than people who don't. They simply have more (and more frequent) chances for contact. At this point let's make very clear what we mean by *promiscuous*. The word has a bad press because it is so often associated with sexual activities that many people regard as improper, abnormal, wicked, or bad. The trouble is, getting the word *promiscuous* all scrambled up with ideas about "good" and "bad" behavior confuses a lot of people and doesn't help clear up thinking about the disease because the AIDS virus—the real villain in this piece—doesn't understand anything about "good" or "bad" behavior. It will be much more helpful if we stick to the dictionary meaning of *promiscuous:* "having intimate sexual relations with a lot of different people on a casual basis." If we take *promiscuous* to mean just that and nothing more, then we could say that the approximate opposite would be *monogamous*, meaning "having intimate sexual relations essentially with just one person—or at least with very few."

Among the sexually promiscuous people who are at exceptionally high risk, one group is obviously those male homosexuals who engage in sexual relations with many partners. This is one of the groups in which HIV first appeared and spread widely in this country, so among these people there is a large pool of infected persons capable of spreading the disease. It is important to recognize that the problem with this group is *not their homosexuality;* it is the promiscuous sexual practices that many of them engage in. Among the male homosexuals who have never been promiscuous, but have had essentially long-term, monogamous relationships, AIDS has *not* been present. When it *has* appeared among these people, it has usually been found that one partner or the other has been having some promiscuous sexual experience outside the monogamous relationship.

Interestingly enough, female homosexuals who confine their sexual activity exclusively to other females *don't get AIDS infections.* As far as has been reported so far, there has not been a single case of AIDS in a lesbian woman who has not had sex contacts with men and who is not an intravenous drug user. As for promiscuous male homosexuals, it is believed that they are at such an extraordinarily high risk of contracting AIDS—at least in part—because of the common practice of anal intercourse. This practice often results in abrasion and bleeding of the rectal mucous membrane and can therefore lead to exposure not only to infected semen but to infected blood as well.

Female prostitutes are, by definition, engaged in promiscuous sexual activity and are thus another group at extraordinarily high risk of contracting AIDS. Adding to their risk is the fact that many female prostitutes are also intravenous drug users. These people, if infected, obviously subject their clients—usually heterosexual males—to a high risk of contracting AIDS. If future experience continues to show an increasing spread of AIDS through male-female sex contacts, as seems almost certain, then it will follow that people with promiscuous *heterosexual* sex lives are also going to be at much greater risk of AIDS than those who confine their sexual relationships to one or a very few other people. We'll say more about this later.

Intravenous drug users who share needles and injection equipment with others form another group at exceptionally high risk of AIDS because of the large amounts of virus found in the blood of infected individuals. We know there is already a large pool of infected people among these drug users. In fact, this route of infection accounts for even more cases of AIDS in such areas as New York City and northern New Jersey than homosexual contact does. What is more, as we will see, these people create a particularly dangerous "window of infection" to the rest of the world because they can so easily infect their heterosexual sex partners, who may then infect *other* heterosexual sex partners or, most tragic of all in the case of women, infect their babies if they become pregnant.

TRANSFUSION BLOOD AND ANTIBODY TESTING

Early in the AIDS epidemic one other group of people was found to be at exceptionally high risk of contracting the infection: people with hemophilia, a blood-clotting disease, who had to receive frequent transfusions of whole blood or concentrated blood products in order to treat their illness. In the early 1980s more and more hemophiliacs were turning up with full-blown AIDS without any reason other than the blood products they had been receiving—blood that had been donated by AIDS-infected people and obviously was contaminated by the HIV virus. In addition, some cases occurred in people who had simply required blood transfusions during surgery between 1980 and 1984. Today AIDS experts believe that not very much contaminated blood was drawn by blood banks or transfused during that period, but *some* was, and the hemophilics were especially hard hit because they had to have so much blood so often.

Fortunately, this kind of risk has largely been eliminated since early in 1985, when certain screening tests were introduced so that blood banks could identify contaminated blood and destroy it before it could be dispensed. These same screening tests, however, have assumed a much wider importance in the overall fight against AIDS than just protecting our blood supplies. They have made it possible to tell, with a high degree of accuracy, whether any given individual has been infected with HIV or not, regardless of whether any symptoms have appeared.

The main test used today to screen donated blood for evidence of HIV infection is a laboratory exam known as the ELISA test (taken from its full name, *E*nzyme-*l*inked *I*mmuno*s*orbent *A*ssay). It is not a test for HIV itself, but for *antibodies* against HIV in the blood of an infected person. This test will react with a color change in a test tube if a sample of human blood serum added to the reagents contains antibodies against HIV—an indication that the person has been infected by the virus. The ELISA test is both simple and inexpensive. It can be automated, so tests can be performed in large volume, and is now the method of choice for testing donated blood all over the country. It is used by blood banks to screen not only blood donated for transfusions but also blood that is to be used to prepare the specific blood products that hemophilic patients need. It can also be used as a screening test in any situation in which there is suspicion that a given individual might be infected with the virus.

This test is very *sensitive;* that means it will identify almost anyone who has HIV antibodies in the blood. (Doctors speak of such people as *HIV-positive* or *sero-reactive.*) Unfortunately, in rare cases, a *false negative* result turns up—the test misses somebody who really is positive. It also tends to pick up quite a number of people who don't really have HIV antibodies at all—so-called *false positive* results.

Because of this, all blood samples identified by the ELISA test as HIV positive are subjected to another test known as the "Western blot." This test is very *specific:* if it says that HIV antibody is present in the blood, it's *there*—but it tends to miss quite a few. Between the two, however, these tests offer a high degree of protection to recipients of donor blood, and they have been in universal use by blood banks all over the country since March 1985.

What about people who received ordinary blood transfusions before March of 1985? According to the Centers for Disease Control, as many as 29,000 Americans may have acquired HIV infection from blood bank blood before routine antibody screening was started. Some of those people have already developed AIDS, and others will. Many such people have already chosen to be tested to be sure they were not contaminated. And some blood banks have been recalling such people for free testing. Most authorities think the risk to any individual patient was very small—perhaps one contaminated unit of blood out of 500—but of course the risk would be greater in the major AIDS cities and much less in other communities. Only time will tell us how many people were actually affected and who they were.

Routine screening of donor blood has done an excellent job of restoring the safety of our blood bank blood supplies. Many people, however, continue to worry because the two tests used don't offer an absolute guarantee that the donated blood is free of HIV. A very few donors with HIV antibodies can be missed. In addition, there is that "window" between the time of actual infection and the time antibodies first appear; during this interval a donor could inadvertantly be giving contaminated blood and never be identified. Nor is this just an idle concern: A study reported in the *New England Journal of Medicine* for February 25, 1988, actually identifies cases in which this has happened. Finally, in 1988, researchers discovered another threat: small amounts of blood bank blood in major cities were found to be contaminated with another virus, the leukemia virus HTLV-I, that isn't picked up by HIV testing.

Because of these concerns, some patients have wanted to designate their own blood donors on the assumption (possibly incorrect) that the donors they themselves select will not be infected with HIV. Such a system would present blood banks with staggering problems trying to keep all the blood from designated donors and intended for designated recipients sorted out—so many problems, indeed, that the blood banks couldn't continue to operate if everybody insisted on doing it this way. Another possible solution, perhaps more workable, is known as *autologous donation:* the individual provides his or her own blood in advance of the time it is needed (for anticipated surgery, for example). There are ways that a person can accumulate several units of his or her own blood still fresh enough to be used when needed—or it can be frozen for use in later emergencies. But even this procedure places an enormous burden on the blood bank, and is quite expensive as well. Probably mass screening of all donated blood is the most practical form of protection in the long run. This may become much safer as better screening tests are developed. In addition, a search is on for ways to treat donor blood in order to sterilize it before it is given, destroying any and all viruses that might have slipped through the screening procedure. This could be the best long-run solution of all.

THE INCREASING DILEMMA
OF HIV TESTING

Development of the HIV antibody tests was a major step forward in protecting our national blood supply. But these tests have implications far beyond blood banks. Whatever their shortcomings, they offer a reasonably reliable way to determine who is infected by HIV and who isn't, whether symptoms have appeared or not. If an ELISA test is negative, that person can be assumed to be free of HIV (unless he or she has been infected during the past few months, before antibodies can develop). If repeated ELISA tests are positive, and the test is confirmed with a positive Western blot test, that person can be assumed to *have* HIV infection—and thus be able to pass the virus on to others.

You might think that the availability of such testing would clear the air immensely in dealing with a terrible epidemic like AIDS. Instead, it has created a tangle of conflicting problems that no one yet has been able to solve. Testing has opened an enormous can of worms, and now nobody knows what to do with the worms.

Who should be tested? How often or under what circumstances? Should the testing be *voluntary* (done with consent of the person) or *mandatory* (required by law, whether the person likes it or not) or *involuntary* (not required by law, but done without telling the person—a patient admitted to a hospital, for example)? Should the testing be done anonymously (without identifying the person tested) or openly, using the person's name? Who can guarantee that a person's test result will be kept absolutely confidential? Who should have access to the test results? What should those test results be used for—or not used for?

Some of the answers are easy. Nobody argues against the testing of each and every unit of blood bank blood to protect the blood supply, and the keeping of a confidential file of prospective donors who tested HIV-positive by the blood bank for future reference. But most of the answers are not so easy. Some people *want* to be tested—they want to know if they are infected or not. (Interestingly, most such people are from the very lowest risk groups—that is, people who are least likely to be infected.) Other people emphatically do *not* want to be tested—they do *not* want to know. They argue that if they *are* infected there is nothing they can do about it anyway, and they may never actually develop symptoms. (They may or may not want to face the problem of possibly infecting their sex partners, whereas if they *know* they are HIV-positive, they can prevent this tragedy by a change in their behavior.) Other people are extremely nervous, and suspicious, about the ways AIDS testing might be used against them by others. All kinds of discriminatory practices are cropping up not only against those with active symptomatic AIDS, but against those who are HIV-positive (infected) but not yet sick. Some companies want to fire these people from their jobs. Co-workers don't want to work with them. Life insurance companies want to deny them insurance—or charge high-risk premiums. Health insurance companies want to refuse to cover any treatment related to AIDS. The list goes on and on.

Equally important, in many areas there are very real—and unresolvable—conflicts between the greater public health needs of the nation, on one hand, and the civil and constitutional rights of individuals, on the other. Some people say testing should be required in order to get a marriage license. There is certainly a precedent here; for years, many states required blood tests for syphilis before issuing marriage licenses. Some say all health workers should be tested, or all patients admitted to hospitals. Some demand testing of all homosexuals, or all intravenous drug users, or all convicted prostitutes. These proposals are allegedly for the public good, but without any clear ideas of exactly how those test results should be used. Many AIDS experts think that widespread demands for mandatory testing of special groups is very ominous, and may simply drive many HIV-positive people underground instead of identifying them.

There is one place, however, where widespread testing of some sort *does* make sense—in the area of *surveillance,* learning what the AIDS epidemic is actually doing in a wide population. This is certain to become more and more important to public health as the spread of AIDS among heterosexuals becomes more prominent. In order to learn better how far HIV infection has already penetrated various groups of people in this country who are generally thought to be not at risk, several voluntary mass-testing programs are in the planning stage at this writing. One, for example, will involve anonymous testing of all patients admitted to half a dozen major medical school hospitals over a set period of time. Another program proposes to do testing, on a voluntary basis, of all the students at a major American university who will cooperate with the study. The results of such testing would be used, presumably, solely for study of the epidemic as a whole and not for action regarding individuals. Meanwhile, it appears certain that *some* form of mandatory testing of various groups is surely going to be legislated in various states, for better or for worse. It is equally certain that the problems attending such testing are not going to go away.

THE LOWEST-RISK GROUPS

If we can identify the groups of people who are at exceptionally *high* risk of contracting HIV infections, then we should also be able to identify the groups of people who are at *virtually no risk at all,* at least at the present time and as far as is known. In the simplest possible terms, these practically no-risk groups include:

- people who are not sexually active male homo-sexuals, *and*
- who are not engaged in promiscuous sexual activity, *and*
- who are not intravenous drug users, *and*

- who receive whole blood or blood products only rarely, and then only where blood has been carefully screened against contamination, *and*
- who have never lived in places such as central Africa or Haiti where heterosexual spread of the virus seems to be more common than in the United States.

When you read this list of people who are, at least at present, at little or no risk of acquiring AIDS, it might seem to include the majority of the people reading this book. You might think that most of these people simply don't need to be frightened about possibly acquiring AIDS—*as long as they understand why they are not at risk.*

Unfortunately, you could be wrong. And this brings up a modern-day nightmare: the possibility of HIV infection spreading into low-risk groups through heterosexual sex contact.

Up until the present, most AIDS cases have been confined to people in the very high-risk groups discussed earlier. But right from the beginning there have been a few cases—about 3 or 4 percent of the total—in people who were not in *any* of those high-risk groups. This is not a high *percentage,* but as of December 1987 it included *1400 cases of full-blown, symptomatic AIDS.* And that is a lot of people.

Where did these cases come from? All evidence suggests that most of them came as a result of heterosexual sexual contact.

This should not be surprising. We know that heterosexual spread of the virus is quite common in central Africa and parts of Europe. It just hasn't appeared much—as yet—in supposedly "low-risk" heterosexual populations in the United States. But there are places where the infection can easily "escape" from high-risk groups into the general heterosexual population. Some researchers speak of these areas as "windows of infection" open to the rest of the world.

Bisexual men are one such window of infection. These are people who may have promiscuous sexual contacts with male homosexuals (with very *high* risk of HIV infection) and heterosexual contacts with women as well, placing those women at risk of acquiring the HIV infection from them. These women may then proceed to infect other men, thus carrying the infection to the heterosexual population. Nobody knows how many male bisexuals there are, but there is evidence that quite a number of men practice this sexual lifestyle. And many women may not even know that their male sex partners are, or have been, bisexual—especially women who themselves have had a great many sex partners that they didn't know very well.

Intravenous drug abusers create another major window of infection to the rest of the world. There are hundreds of thousands of these exceedingly high-risk people, with a high percentage already infected with HIV from contaminated injection equipment. These infected ones proceed to infect their sex partners, even though the partners themselves may not be IV drug users. Women infected this way can then infect the babies they carry—a major source of infant AIDS. And if those women have other sex partners, they may infect them as well. Bear in mind that infecting a baby, or a sex partner, can happen years later, when such a woman might have, for example, long since left her drug-using boyfriend, moved to another city and gotten married to a nice young man. She could have changed her life entirely, but nothing could change the HIV virus she carries with her.

Female prostitutes provide yet another window for infection. These women obviously have many sexual contacts, largely with heterosexual men. Many are also intravenous drug users, using prostitution to pay for their drugs. In some areas (New York, New Jersey, Florida, or San Francisco, for example) as many as 45 percent of prostitutes tested have HIV antibodies; in other areas the percentage is much smaller. But any HIV-infected prostitute can transmit the infection to her heterosexual male customer—who may then take it home to his wife or to any other sexual partner he may have. And this is a way that the virus can *really* escape into the low-risk world.

So far there is not much evidence of *increasing* spread of HIV infection in the heterosexual community, nor of *rapid* increase in active AIDS cases. But these people are not generally tested for antibodies, and symptomatic AIDS may not appear for years after infection. Public health officials are highly concerned that we *will* begin seeing rapid increases here very soon unless the whole population is warned and educated and begins taking protective measures.

SOME QUESTIONS AND ANSWERS ABOUT AIDS

Obviously there are a number of things to be worried about where AIDS is concerned, and a great many people are quite legitimately worried and frightened. Unfortunately, a great many low-risk people are frightened of things they don't need to be frightened about, for completely pointless reasons. Probably this is inevitable when a new, mysterious, and deadly disease has appeared that many people don't understand very well. After all, there are sizable numbers of people walking around who are carrying a deadly virus with them. Isn't it terribly risky for the rest of the world to be anywhere near them? The answer is no, it isn't. Nor is there any point wasting energy worrying about things that don't need to be worried about. To deal with some of these unnecessary fears and worries, let's consider some of the questions that many people have been asking about AIDS.

Q. Isn't it true that nobody really knows much about AIDS?

A. No, it's not. That may have been true back in 1981 when the disease first surfaced, but since then AIDS has been studied more intensively than any other disease in history. According to Eddie Hedrick, manager of infection control at the University of Missouri Hospital in Columbia, "Virtually all our questions about AIDS have been answered except how to cure it and how to make a vaccine to prevent it." And one of the things we know the *most* about, he added, is how it's transmitted and who is—and isn't—at risk.*

Q. What about casual, everyday contact with somebody who has AIDS? Is it possible to contract the infection just from being around them?

A. No. As far as AIDS experts know today, it just doesn't happen. Why not? Let's recall some of the facts we already know about the HIV virus. Although it is a

---

*[Ed. note - quotation from *Common Sense About AIDS/January 1988*, copyright 1987 American Health Consultants Inc., 67 Peachtree Park Drive N.E., Atlanta, GA 30309]

very dangerous virus once it gets inside a person's body and starts multiplying, it isn't a very hardy virus at all outside the body. In fact, it is quite frail. It doesn't survive floating around in the air of a room. It doesn't survive long when deposited on hard objects such as doorknobs, toilet seats, or eating utensils. It is very effectively destroyed by most common detergents and disinfectants, including ordinary soap-and-water washing of the hands. People who have AIDS are not shedding viruses into the environment as they walk around. The virus is not spread by coughing or sneezing or respiratory droplets the way cold and flu viruses are. You aren't going to acquire an AIDS infection from an infected person unless you have sexual contact with him or her, or are in intimate contact with that person's infected blood or other body fluids.

The truth of this is borne out by some plain facts that have been observed and recorded in medical journals. For example, to date there have been no known cases of transmission of AIDS from an infected person to other members of the family—children, brothers or sisters, aunts or uncles, wives or husbands—except where sexual intimacy has been involved or where some other truly extraordinary contact with the infected person's body fluids has occurred. For instance, there was one celebrated case reported in which a mother acquired AIDS while caring for her hemophilic son who had acquired AIDS from contaminated blood products. But in this case the child was exceedingly ill, and had bloody diarrhea which the mother was continually having to clean up. She did so repeatedly without wearing protective gloves of any sort, and ultimately became infected—

hardly an ordinary case. One study, which appeared in the *New England Journal of Medicine* in February 1986, reported that even long-term household contact with AIDS patients in a large sampling of cases didn't produce even any sign of antibodies in the blood of family members, much less any symptoms of AIDS.

There *is* evidence that the infection *can* be spread through much-closer-than-casual (although not sexually intimate) contact with AIDS patients. For example, a handful of hospital workers have acquired the infection as a result of contact with blood from hospitalized AIDS patients. Most of these cases have been the result of accidental needle pricks, but two cases involved spilling or splashing a sample of the patient's blood. Such contacts are tragic, but they are not *common*. Recognizing the potential hazard, the CDC has recommended that hospitals and laboratories take "universal precautions" with all patients' blood and body fluids, both in patient rooms and in surgeries. Such precautions, such as wearing rubber gloves when drawing blood samples, will make such accidental contacts even more rare.

What does this mean in terms of the everyday lives of people who have AIDS—and people who come in contact with them? According to the doctors who know the most about the disease, it means that a person infected with AIDS who works in an office is not going to transmit AIDS to other office workers by casual contact. It means that a child with AIDS is not going to transmit the infection to classmates in school. It means that a person with AIDS is not going to infect others in the family by everyday household contact. One of the great tragedies of this disease is that on top of the burden of having a terrible, fatal disease, people with AIDS also have the burden of being treated like modern-day lepers—and there is no rational reason, as far as we know today, for that to be happening.

Q. What about other kinds of contacts? What about kissing a person with AIDS? Isn't it possible that body fluids such as saliva, tears, or perspiration might be infective?

A. Such a thing is conceivable, but as far as is known today, it just doesn't happen. We know that an infected person's blood, the semen in the male, and the vaginal secretions in the female, can contain large quantities of the virus and has to be considered dangerously infective. This is borne out by the fact that many, many cases are known to have been transmitted by these routes. As for saliva, we know that some viruses, such as the Epstein-Barr (EB) virus—a herpes virus that causes infectious mononucleosis, are present in large quantities in the saliva of an infected person, and that kissing may be a major factor in the spread of *that* infection. But this does not seem to be the case with HIV. When HIV is found in the saliva at all, it is in very small quantities. In a study reported in the *New England Journal of Medicine* in January 1986, doctors at Massachusetts General Hospital in Boston tested both blood and saliva in some seventy-eight patients with full-blown AIDS. The live HIV virus was found in the blood of the vast majority of those patients, but in the saliva of only one. This would suggest that the chance a person might be infected just by kissing a person with full-blown AIDS is extremely small— about equivalent to the risk of being struck dead by lightning while walking down the street. It could happen, but it's not something reasonable people would ordinarily worry about. The same can be said for contact with tears, perspiration or urine—body fluids in which HIV is known *not* to concentrate.

The situation is a little different in the case of dentists or dental hygienists who spend all day long, day after day, with their fingers in the mouths of a lot of different people about whom they may know very little. Today many of these professionals prefer to wear face masks and rubber gloves as a protective measure, and no one should be offended. Based on today's knowledge, this is probably a simple, harmless, and sensible precaution for them to take. Carried to the other extreme, there are people who are fearful of taking Holy Communion from a common communion cup for fear of contracting AIDS. This is probably an unreasonable fear; however, most churches that normally employ a common communion chalice offer some alternative way of taking communion for those who are concerned.

Q. What about waiters, bartenders, and food handlers? Shouldn't they be required to be tested to be sure they don't have AIDS?

A. Again, there has never been a single reported case of AIDS being transmitted by these people in the normal course of their work. And if you are going to require that *they* be tested, what about other people? Fishermen? Farmers? Meat packers? Bus drivers? Airline pilots? Laundry workers? Where are you going to stop? We already have rational laws to enforce proper hygiene for food handlers (washing the hands after use of the toilet, for example) as a commonsense public health measure against food-borne diseases. Probably the appearance of AIDS is an excellent reason for extremely careful enforcement of these normal hygienic procedures—but there is no evidence to date that anyone in this group who has AIDS would be a threat to the public in the course of his or her normal duties.

Q. Can people get AIDS from mosquito bites?

A. Not as far as is known. This idea popped up from a cluster of AIDS cases that occurred in Belle Glade, Florida. Since the victims didn't seem to have high-risk behavior, mosquitos were suspected. But CDC investigators concluded that mosquitos had nothing to do with it. Among other things, all of the cases were found in sexually active adults or infant babies; *not one case* occurred in children between the ages of five and fifteen. Surely they, too, would have been affected if mosquitos were the carriers. And later studies deliberately set up to test the "mosquito theory" elsewhere have gotten nowhere.

Q. I've heard that you can get AIDS by donating blood. How could this be true?

A. It *couldn't* be true, and it staggers the imagination to guess where this false idea might have come from, but unfortunately a lot of people believe it. The truth is, of course, that there is *absolutely no risk whatever* of getting AIDS from giving blood. Nothing but brand-new, sterile, one-time-use needles, tubing and bags are ever used. There is no imaginable way that a person could acquire AIDS by donating blood.

Q. You keep saying "as far as we know" AIDS can't be spread by casual contact—but what if we really *don't* know, and later it turns out that experts are wrong about this? Wouldn't it be much safer for everybody if people who had AIDS were quarantined so they couldn't possibly spread it to anyone else?

A. As a matter of fact this has been proposed, out of fear and panic. But consider the terrible social consequences of such a program. What sort of "quarantine" would be required? Herding people into concentration camps? Who would be placed there? It would have to include not only people with full-blown AIDS but anybody who even had a positive antibody test for AIDS, including many people with false positive tests. CDC estimates that there are already 1,500,000 such people in the country. So how would you quarantine them all? Would you agree to pay the staggering extra taxes necessary to support them? And if so, how would all these people be identified? Should everybody in the country be required to have an antibody test? Would *you* care to submit to a test if you might be quarantined as a result?

Even more terrible questions would arise. Who would decide who would be quarantined and who wouldn't? Who would you like to have administering such a program? Who would protect us from the people—or groups of people—who would like to use the widespread fear of AIDS as an excuse to attack homosexuals, or prostitutes, or anyone else they think might have "questionable" sexual inclinations or practices—or just anyone who *disagreed* with them—in order to "protect society?"

Such a program isn't necessary to "protect society," according to the best medical advice we have. It couldn't possibly work without creating a vast police state to enforce it, and probably not even then. Far better that people should learn to *protect themselves,* to devote their energies to learning what is true about AIDS and finding rational ways to prevent its spread.

Certainly we see a picture emerging of a terrible and potentially deadly new disease which has afflicted thousands upon thousands of people—in every state in the Union—and has already become the most urgent public health concern in history. Its spread has already reached epidemic proportions and shows no sign of slowing down. The worst is yet to come.

But we also see a picture of a disease that is not just spreading willy-nilly. It is spreading in specific, clearly recognized ways. It is also *not* spreading in certain other ways in which many more familiar virus diseases spread.

Surely anybody who has any awareness of this disease would like to be as sure as possible that he or she does not contract it. And fortunately, from what we know about this disease, it is possible to outline a number of things that any thinking person can do to guard against the infection.

CHAPTER SEVEN

HOW TO PROTECT YOURSELF AGAINST AIDS

During the 1960s and 1970s a widespread and very real revolution took place in the way that young people, from junior high on up through high school and college, went about living their lives.

Many young people today find it almost impossible to believe how things were back in the 1940s and 1950s, before that revolution took place. In those days, of course, large numbers of young people started smoking cigarettes as early as junior high age, often ending up in big fights with their parents about this, even though many of their parents also smoked cigarettes. Quite a few also had their first acquaintance with alcohol at about that age, most commonly with beer. But tobacco and alcohol were really the beginning and end of the "drug scene" among young people in those days. Very few had even heard of marijuana, much less tried it. Speed and downers—amphetamines and barbiturates or tranquilizers—were practically unheard of. Few had ever *seen* heroin. Kids knew about addiction to things like heroin, but nobody dreamed of using it, and most would have recoiled in horror at the idea of sticking a needle into their arms and injecting a drug into their veins. They knew it happened, of course, but certainly not among *them.*

Young people's attitudes towards sex relations (or at least toward actual sexual intimacy and sexual intercourse) were far more simple and innocent in those days, too. For most kids, "real sex" was considered pretty much off limits. There was a lot of necking and petting, but actual sexual intercourse was rare, usually confined to couples who had paired off as "steadies." Promiscuous sex—with lots of different partners, more or less casually—just wasn't well regarded. The few girls who engaged in it were well known and marked by their classmates, and while the boys did a lot of bragging, for the most part it was just bragging. The *venereal,* or sexually transmitted, diseases were uncommon among kids in the forties and fifties, and although an occasional girl would inadvertently become pregnant, it was a matter of this one and that one, not an epidemic.

The revolution of the 1960s and 1970s changed all this among many young people. Tobacco and alcohol use continued, but marijuana became the rage, and speed and downers became widely available and widely used. Presently those "recreational drugs" were joined by cocaine (for those who could afford it)—and quite a number of young people had experience with injectable narcotic drugs. Of course parents and teachers and other "adult authorities" fought bitterly against this trend, but they couldn't really do much about it. To many young people, participating in the drug scene was a new-found "freedom."

The same could be said for sex relations. In the 1960s and 1970s adolescents began intimate sexual explorations more and more widely at younger and younger ages, with more approval and sanction from their peers than ever before. Many family, religious, and social restraints seemed to be lifted. After all, young people reached physical and sexual maturity between the ages of twelve and fourteen, and when their gonads began vibrating, why not respond to them? There was a popular perception that authority figures, especially parents, were old stick-in-the-muds in this matter; who was to say that young people shouldn't engage in any degree of sexual activity they chose? And who was to stop them? To many young people this increased sexual awareness and activity became regarded as another newfound "freedom." The boys stopped just boasting and, among girls, the social curiosity or outcast was no longer the girl who had sex with every boy in class but rather the girl who didn't.

Of course, along with these exciting new-found freedoms regarding drug use and sex came a few other perhaps less desirable freedoms: the freedom, for example, to get your head thoroughly scrambled up, and maybe your life as well, by drug dependencies; the freedom to have an unwanted pregnancy at the age of fourteen or fifteen or even younger, a development that began to reach epidemic proportions in high schools and even junior highs; the freedom to contract a variety of interesting sexually transmitted diseases, including gonorrhea, syphilis, and genital herpes; and now, in the 1980s, yet another "delight"—the freedom to become infected with the HIV virus of AIDS. But while drug dependencies, unwanted pregnancies, and most other sexually transmitted diseases were undesirable, they were not generally lethal. Infection with the AIDS virus can be very lethal indeed.

THE CONCEPT OF
DEFENSIVE LIVING

Like everyone else, a great many young people from time to time make foolish decisions, do foolish things, and occasionally take foolish risks. But most of them are not stupid, and when faced with a very real threat such as AIDS, most can see the sense in trying to protect themselves, provided they have some plain-facts guidelines to follow.

Perhaps the most important element for self-protection is to recognize that *each individual is personally vulnerable,* and that each individual must be responsible for protecting himself or herself first, before worrying about anybody else. This may seem an extremely selfish attitude to take, but the fact is that the person who is in terrible trouble because of an HIV infection is the person who contracts it—nobody else. And nobody else is going to protect you because nobody else but *you* can make the necessary decisions for your own protection. If any protecting is going to be done, you are the one who is going to have to do it.

This idea was discussed at length in a *Journal of the American Medical Association* editorial by Dr. George Lundberg. After discussing what we know about how AIDS is transmitted from person to person, and what few defenses society as a whole has against its spread, Dr. Lundberg concluded: "It may behoove those people who do not wish to get AIDS to adjust their life-styles so as to practice living defensively—particularly in the sexual arena. Individuals have the power to protect themselves more than science currently can."* And this may prove to be especially excellent advice if we find (as we well may) that AIDS is spreading more widely through conventional heterosexual intimacy than has been the case up to now. This hasn't happened on a wide scale *yet,* but scientists everywhere recognize that it is a very real possibility, and many are virtually certain that it *will* happen, sooner or later.

There is no question that the next five years will add a great deal to our knowledge and experience with AIDS and will tell us much more than we now know about how to adjust our ways of living in terms of self-protection. In the meantime, "living defensively" does not mean going into a panic or being pointlessly frightened. It simply means using the things that we know—the facts that we have—about AIDS and its spread to help us make decisions for our own best interests. Let's look at these things one by one.

INTRAVENOUS DRUG ABUSE

We know that people who use illicit intravenous drugs are at very high risk of contracting AIDS, and the more frequent and regular the use, the higher the risk. Here self-protective measures are obvious, simple, and straight-forward. If you are already in that high-risk group, get out of it; if you are not yet a person in this high-risk group, see that you never get into it. Nobody *has* to start using cocaine or injecting heroin or other street drugs. Even if the pressures to do so may be very great at one time or another, if you recognize that

---

*George Lundberg, "The Age of AIDS: A Great Time for Defensive Living," *Journal of the American Medical Association* (June 21, 1985).

those pressures are truly malignant—absolutely against your best interests in every possible way—then you have identified the enemy and know whom to keep away from in order to protect yourself. Nobody who already uses these injectable drugs has to continue using them unless he or she is addicted—and even the addicted can find medical help to overcome the addiction and get away from this risk of contracting AIDS. It isn't easy, but it is possible; thousands of people have done it. Wherever you stand, the self-protective rule is plain: If you're not in this risk group, don't get into it, and if you are in it, get out of it as fast as possible.

Avoiding intravenous drug abuse is not only great self-protection for you but a benefit to society as well, because it can help reduce one of the largest reservoirs of the virus that there is in this country and one of the most difficult to even begin to eliminate by public health efforts or scientific breakthroughs. How important this may be for the future is just beginning to become clear. Some very recent statistics indicate that the rapid increase in new cases of AIDS among male homosexuals may be slowing down or leveling off slightly, whereas there is no sign of any such trend in the New York-New Jersey area, where intravenous drug users are a major reservoir of infection. Researchers suspect that these differences may be occurring because many members of the male homosexual community have begun altering or modifying their sexual practices voluntarily, as a matter of self-protection. But where intravenous drug abuse is widespread, this risk element far outweighs any changes in the habits or sexual practices among homosexuals. So the galloping increase in the numbers of new cases in the intravenous drug group is continuing unabated, and will go right on continuing unless intravenous drug abuse is reduced, one individual at a time.

In addition, intravenous drug abusers represent a particularly dangerous window of infection to the general heterosexual population, as we saw in chapter six. Many of these people, infected with HIV, can pass the infection on to their heterosexual sex partners, and those partners can pass it on to others. Thus AIDS experts believe that *anything* that will help reduce the number of intravenous drug users will, in the long run, help curb the wildfire spread of this disease.

SEXUAL PRACTICES AND LIFE-STYLES

We have seen that certain sexual practices and ways of living are associated with a very high risk of contracting AIDS, while certain others carry little or no risk of AIDS. Obviously, then, a major step in self-protection against infection would be to live a very defensive sexual life—that is, to confine yourself to known low-risk sexual practices and life-styles if possible, and if you are already involved in a high-risk pattern of sexual behavior, make deliberate changes to reduce the risk as quickly as possible.

In this regard, even though the preponderance of AIDS cases up to now has appeared in male homosexuals, the whole question of sexual orientation is nothing but a red herring when it comes to pursuing a self-protective, defensive sexual life-style for yourself. We are not talking here about homosexual versus heterosexual, with bisexual thrown into the middle somewhere. HIV is a *sexually-transmitted virus* and the virus doesn't know homosexual from heterosexual or bisexual. It is the *individual's sexual behavior pattern* that puts him or her at high risk or low risk, not the sexual orientation. Bearing this in mind, there are a number of low-risk, defensive sexual patterns available:

Celibacy or abstinence. This means no sexual relations at all with anybody else. If we are talking about a virus that is primarily transmitted by sexual contact, then abstinence is obviously about as low risk as you can get. For the many churches and other religious and ethical groups that encourage sexual abstinence until marriage, the threat of AIDS is just one more valid reason to adhere to these teachings. True enough, for many people, including a great many young people, *indefinite* celibacy is not very practical, livable, workable, or desirable as a long-term commitment. Yet for certain limited time periods, or under certain circumstances, maybe it is. One thing is certain: if you decide not to have sex relations with anybody at all for some period of time as a matter of self-protection, and then *don't,* you are not going to inadvertently contract AIDS from someone through sexual contact. This is probably the best kind of protection you can find.

Nobody can make this kind of decision for you. In a sense you really *do* have a "new-found freedom" that you alone can exercise—the freedom to decide *not to,* for the time being, for reasons that are good and sufficient to yourself, including your own self-protection. It is true that many young people today regard sex as entertainment, or athletic exercise, or as a way of accepting people they like very much, or simply as something they enjoy because it feels good. But these young people, as individuals living defensively in dangerous times, might want to consider that there are other kinds of entertainment, other athletic outlets, other ways of accepting people, or other things that feel good, and that merely feeling good for a short time through sex relations just may not be worth the risk. When, at some time, you combine sex with an enduring, loving relationship with another person— with a lasting emotional commitment and a sharing of other aspects of your life and feelings with another person—then sexual activity becomes irresistible. But for a great many young people this kind of broad-spectrum combination of sex with love and commitment and sharing doesn't actually exist yet and has very little to do with the popular "sexual revolution." For many, "celibacy for the time being" might be the most sensible of all self-protective measures.

Promiscuity versus monogamy. While abstinence can be a good protective option to consider on a temporary basis, the fact is that it isn't very realistic for the long term for most people. The question then becomes, what kinds of sexual life-styles make the most sense in terms of living defensively and what kinds don't? Again, what we already know about AIDS provides some pretty good answers. We have seen that the person who has frequent and repeated sexual contacts with lots of partners day after day has a far greater risk of contracting AIDS than the person who has less frequent sexual contact with only a few different partners. Monogamous sexual contact with only one partner is the least risky of all sexual life-styles. Indeed, all observations so far indicate that stable, long-term, single-partner relationships between males and females without any sexual contact outside this configuration seem to be almost totally free of the risk of contracting AIDS. And certain specific kinds of sexual contact, such as anal intercourse, seem significantly more risky than, say, oral sex between homosexuals or vaginal sexual contacts between heterosexual couples.

Basically, these are the facts that have been widely observed and scientifically recorded up to the present time. They aren't guesswork, or unsupported opinion, or an attempt to frighten or coerce people; they are just the facts. Anyone who is interested in living defensively should consider these facts carefully in reaching a decision about what kind of sexual life-style—which sexual behavior pattern—makes the most sense for him or her.

Self-protection in risk situations. Clearly, it would be helpful—and self-protective—if a person who already has a high-risk sexual life-style could at least modify it to make it less risky. Just how helpful such modification can be has been documented in most depth in the male homosexual communities of San Francisco, Miami, and New York.

There is evidence, for example, that casual and heedless sexual promiscuity has been losing its charm and acceptance in these communities, as it has become more and more evident that these practices are a clear and present threat to the very lives of the people involved. Many of these men are choosing to moderate the number and frequency of their sexual contacts. Some are, by their own histories, withdrawing to celibate life-styles, at least temporarily. Others are certainly weighing the risks of their life-styles more carefully and rationally than ever before. The public bathhouses, for example, which were previously among the most popular locales for promiscuous sexual contact, are becoming less popular; and the attitude in many bars frequented by male homosexuals, once primarily places to make sexual contacts, is turning more and more to consideration of ways that members of the community can protect themselves. And already there is preliminary evidence that these changes are having positive effects, that the number of new cases of AIDS among homosexual men in some areas is beginning to level off.

One very simple precaution can help such protective efforts succeed, and can be applied to *any* kind of sexual contact that might be the least bit questionable: use of a simple latex rubber condom or sheath on the penis during sexual contact. Condoms are widely and inexpensively available and have been used for years as a means not only of preventing unwanted pregnancies but also as a protection against many sexually transmitted diseases. Used during sexual contact, condoms protect against direct physical touching; if they proved impenetrable to the AIDS virus, their use could be a great protection. And recently several careful and detailed medical studies have indicated that latex rubber condoms actually do prevent penetration of the HIV virus.* (So-called "natural" condoms made of sheep gut cannot be counted upon for this purpose.)

Certainly in the case of high-risk sexual contacts, including those involving anal intercourse, the routine use of a condom can provide a very real measure of protection. Promotion of this idea by responsible leaders in various homosexual communities has been one of the most heartening of all public responses to the AIDS dilemma, even though it has encountered

---

American Medical News. P. 42. January 27, 1986.

some perfectly ridiculous problems along the way. One university health center in San Francisco, for instance, began providing individually wrapped condoms free of charge for distribution in homosexual bars in the vicinity. After passing out about sixty thousand condoms in this way, they received a phone call from the local Food and Drug Administration (FDA) office demanding that they stop calling these devices "condoms." "Condoms," according to the FDA, could refer only to protective sheaths used during vaginal intercourse, not for homosexual use. Call them anything they chose, the FDA said—call them "intimate apparel" or "designer underthings," or "protective barriers," or anything else they wanted—but don't call them "condoms!"

Many medical authorities on AIDS today believe that the widespread use of condoms during any remotely questionable sexual contacts—homosexual, heterosexual, or any other kind—could prove to be one of our most powerful means of preventing the spread of this disease. Even Dr. C. Everett Koop, the Surgeon General of the United States, has endorsed this means of protection, although he emphasizes that abstinence, for young people, is far more desirable a protection. Whether other types of direct physical protection—the use, for example, of spermicidal foams or jellies—can also provide protection has not yet been fully investigated or reported on, but it surely will be in the future.

One should not get the idea, however, that use of condoms is the perfect protection against AIDS—far from it. Condoms are only a barrier to virus contact. They will not work if they are not used consistently and regularly, and they will not work if they are not used *correctly.* If they aren't used soon enough, if they are put on incorrectly, or torn, or slip off during intercourse, all protection is lost. Here are some basic rules for using a condom correctly for self-protection:*

1. Use a condom *every single time* you have sex.

2. The man should put on the condom as soon as his penis is erect, before he has *any* contact with the partner's genital area.

3. Roll the condom all the way down to the base of the penis before starting sex.

4. Coat the condom with spermicidal jelly or foam before sex. This will make the outside slippery and keep the condom from tearing. *Don't* use vaseline or vegetable oil for this. These things break down the rubber.

5. The man should pull his penis out soon after climax, before it gets soft, holding onto the rim of the condom so it doesn't slip off. That way there won't be any unprotected contact.

6. Don't use the same condom more than once.

7. To be extra safe, the woman should also put a spermicide into her vagina before sex. The spermicide may provide extra protection against infection, although this hasn't been clearly proven yet.

---

*Adapted from Robert Hatcher, *Contraceptive Technology 1986-1987,* ed. 13. (New York: Irvington Publishers, 1987) and Marsha F. Goldsmith, "Medical News and Perspectives," *Journal of the American Medical Association,* May 1, 1987, Vol 257, No 17.

Only time will tell us how much impact these guidelines for protective living may ultimately have on slowing down the spread of AIDS. But even a deadly disease like this follows certain rules. If we understand the rules well enough, then we can protect ourselves, individually, against the disease. Meanwhile, research is going on at a furious pace to increase our knowledge of "the rules," to find other possible ways to block the spread of the disease and, in time, to help those people who have become infected.

CHAPTER EIGHT

WHAT THE FUTURE HOLDS

Up to this point, our discussion of AIDS has been grim in just about every dimension. We are dealing with a new disease that appeared very suddenly and is spreading very rapidly. There is real concern that the original population of potential victims, confined to certain small minority communities of high risk, may gradually be expanding to a much broader community that could include everybody. We do not know any way to protect ourselves from infection by this virus once we have come in contact with it, nor do we know of any cure for the disease. We don't even know, for sure, of any effective way to modify or arrest the infection once it has occurred. And we know that once the disease has reached a certain clear-cut, full-blown stage it is—so far—invariably fatal.

That's not a nice picture, but at least there are some things to be said on the bright side. There is reason to hope that the future picture will not be as gray as the present. Understanding the nature of the disease has had to come first. When AIDS made its first recognized appearance in the United States in 1981, it was a totally baffling mystery. But in just seven years an enormous amount has been learned about it. Today we have a whole army of doctors and other researchers working vigorously to extend that knowledge and to find answers to some very tough questions. Where did the HIV virus come from, and why did it make such an abrupt appearance? What is the full story of how this virus behaves once it has invaded cells in the human body? How does it do its damage to the immune system and the nervous system, and why is it so selectively interested in lymphocytes and brain cells? Why does it cause such widely different early symptoms in different people? What other tissues or organ systems may it also attack, perhaps without our knowledge? Will there be people who are infected but never do develop full-blown, fatal AIDS? If so, why? And what other still-unsuspected long-term side effects of the infection, if any, may those people suffer sooner or later?

Above all, three pressing questions have priority in AIDS research today: How can we effectively treat patients who have AIDS? Will there ever be a way to cure it? And how can people be protected against this infection in the first place?

These questions are being studied in clinics, hospitals, and research centers all over the world in one of the largest research efforts in all medical history. Some of the answers are already beginning to appear. Others may come quickly; hardly a month goes by without new discoveries reported about this disease. But some other answers—perhaps the most important ones—may still be a long time in coming.

THE QUESTION
OF TREATMENT

Five years ago at a medical conference, when the
desperate nature of the AIDS epidemic was just
becoming clear, an AIDS expert from the Centers for
Disease Control in Atlanta was asked point-blank
what possible treatments for AIDS were under investigation at that time. His reply: "We are grabbing at
straws, right now."

Now, five years later, doctors are still grabbing at
straws, and there is still no known cure—but at least
there are a few straws to grab at.

The most obvious place to look for a cure might
seem to be in the area of antiviral drugs that could kill
the HIV virus, or at least slow down its attack on the
body in some way. There *are* a few drugs known to be
at least partially effective against other viruses. For
example, a drug called Acyclovir can interfere enough
with the reproduction of the genital herpes virus HSV-
2 to shorten the duration and slow down the recurrences of genital herpes quite markedly in an infected
person. Doctors learned early on that Acyclovir, used
alone, had almost no effect on the AIDS virus—but
perhaps some other antiviral drug might.

Just such a drug, called azidothymidine, or AZT,
came under close scrutiny in the mid-1980s. The drug
appeared to slow or stop the replication of HIV in
laboratory cell cultures, and testing in human AIDS
patients began with great urgency. AZT was not a
cure, by any means. But in prolonged use it did make
AIDS patients feel better, reduce the number and
severity of their opportunistic infections and—most
important—it seemed to slow the downward spiral of

the illness and prolong the lives of many of the seriously ill for months or even years.

AZT was clearly a major step forward in treatment, and the Food and Drug Administration (FDA) broke records in approving it for use in very sick AIDS patients in 1986. But there were problems.

For one thing, AZT is extremely *toxic,* causing some very harsh and often dangerous side effects. In many patients the high doses necessary every four hours around the clock cause severe nausea and vomiting. Worse yet, the drug depresses the bone marrow so severely that repeated blood transfusions are often necessary for people taking the medicine. Many patients just can't tolerate the drug at all.

Second, AZT was in very short supply and strictly rationed. It was also extremely expensive, costing a patient some $10,000 a year when it was first released. Today the supply of the drug is somewhat more adequate, and under extreme social pressure the drug's manufacturer has finally reduced the price about 25 percent, but it is still a severe financial burden for any AIDS patient.

Today AZT—now renamed *zidovudine*—is being used by many severely ill AIDS patients. But many questions remain to be answered. Will this drug also be effective—perhaps even more effective, in smaller doses—for patients with the earlier, less devastating symptoms of ARC? Could it prevent such persons from ever developing full-blown AIDS, with its opportunistic infections or cancers? Could it perhaps greatly slow down the progress of the infection or even arrest it—stop it in its tracks—even if it can't cure it? What about people who are HIV-positive, infected with the virus but not yet showing any symptoms at all? Could AZT prevent symptoms indefinitely in such people? At this time these critical questions have not yet been answered. One thing is sure, however—there is a great demand for the drug, with or without a doctor's prescription. Everyone with symptomatic AIDS wants to take it if they can, and a black market for the drug has already appeared.

Meanwhile, a whole list of other drugs are under investigation for possible anti-HIV effectiveness. Two of these—a body protein product known as *alpha-interferon* and another called *Interleukin 2*—have been found to exhibit some antiviral effects in the body under some circumstances, and might—at least in theory—have some effect to modify the progress of AIDS by attacking the virus's replication. Another such product, a hormone called *thymosin,* might work in a different way, possibly helping the body replenish T-helper lymphocytes. These substances are all currently being studied in patients with AIDS.

A number of other drugs aimed at these two major goals—either attacking the virus itself, or seeking to help the body recover its lost immune protection in some way—are under urgent investigation. For example, one such drug known as AL-721 is already being taken by AIDS patients even though tests for safety and effectiveness have not been completed and the FDA has not approved widespread use of this experimental drug. Desperate people are not willing to wait for slow-moving governmental processes to unfold while they themselves are dying. This and other drugs may or may not prove to be helpful, in the long run. Possibly combinations may help. There is some evidence, for example, that AZT combined with Acyclovir may be more helpful than AZT alone, or may make lower, less toxic doses of AZT possible.

This progress in drug treatment research has raised a totally different question: what about prophylactic—that is, preventive—treatment? With no cure for AIDS in sight, with such high mortality rates for those who get it, and with no vaccine yet available, what is the possibility of using drugs prophylactically, before symptoms appear, to escape the effects of infection? What would happen, for instance, if *everybody* who tested HIV-positive could start taking a drug, or combination of drugs, to prevent the disease from developing? Obviously, this could be a serious consideration, given the right drugs. AZT in full dosage as we know it now might not work because of its severe toxicity—but it is possible that somewhat lower doses might work prophylactically at an early stage of infection. Conceivably other drugs, perhaps as yet undiscovered, might work even better. Only time will tell how practical (or successful) this idea may prove to be.

Meanwhile, a search continues for new ways to treat the opportunistic infections and cancers that actually kill patients with full-blown AIDS eventually. Fortunately, cancers such as Kaposi's sarcoma and lymphoma can be arrested, at least temporarily, with already-known modes of cancer treatment such as chemotherapy or radiation. But treatment of opportunistic infections is a more difficult problem. One trouble is that these infections have never, in the past, been of any great interest to researchers developing antibiotic drugs or antiprotozoan chemicals because the infections occurred so seldom. As a result, now when we really *need* such drugs, there aren't very many available or they don't work very well. For example, until recently there has been only one drug combination (trimethoprim and sulfamethoxazole) really effective against *Pneumocystis carinii* pneumonia, but it becomes less and less effective as the patient has recurrent bouts of the infection and many people begin having bad side effects from it. Now another drug, pentamidine, works against PCP in some patients. Other drugs, such as the antifungal antibiotics sometimes used in treating candidiasis, are even less effective in AIDS patients. But there is hope that researchers, now under the pressure of real need, will find more effective alternatives to these drugs as time goes on. It is this hope, of course, that explains why doctors are working so hard trying to keep AIDS patients alive even though they know that they are soon going to die anyway. As one doctor put it, "The purpose of treating each infection as it comes along is to prolong life, so that when and if a real cure for AIDS is discovered, those patients who are still alive can benefit from the labor of many scientists."

THE QUESTION OF VACCINES

Of course, trying to treat AIDS after a person is infected is like locking the barn after the horse is stolen. By far the best way to deal with this deadly virus would be to prevent infection altogether—and that means finding a safe, effective vaccine. As Dr. Robert Gallo, co-discoverer of the AIDS virus, said recently in an interview, "If we don't find a vaccine, we will have this disease with us forever."*

So far there is no such vaccine available that can be given to a person before infection to protect against HIV. A major research effort is under way to develop such a vaccine, but staggering problems must be solved, and it will almost certainly be several years before any such vaccine becomes available for general use.

Why the problems, and why so long? To make such a vaccine, it is first necessary to find some protein portion of the virus that is absolutely safe to inject into people without any risk of causing an actual AIDS infection. But that safe protein, once injected, must also be able to stimulate formation of anti-HIV antibodies that will actually kill or immobilize live AIDS viruses that might get into the body later. So far, researchers have found a variety of virus proteins that might work, but have no way to tell whether any antibodies formed would actually prevent infection or not. Some of the most successful vaccines against other virus infections (measles, for instance, or polio) use live but *attenuated,* or weakened, viruses for the vaccine— but nobody is enthusiastic about making an AIDS vaccine out of the live virus, no matter how weakened it may be. Unfortunately, however, using a noninfective chunk of virus protein may not create an effective vaccine. Furthermore, there is the question of possible genetic changes or mutation in HIV after a vaccine is made. A second HIV virus, HIV-2, has already been discovered which is different enough from HIV that

---

*Gallo, R. C.: Grand Rounds interview with Dennis L. Breo. *American Medical News,* December 4, 1987.

one vaccine would not be effective against both viruses. A vaccine effective against the present strain of virus would not protect against HIV-2, and might not protect against later mutations either.

An even more formidable obstacle to the development of a vaccine is the problem of testing for safety and effectiveness. Obviously it isn't practical to give human beings an experimental vaccine, deliberately infect them with HIV, and then wait ten years to see if they develop symptoms of AIDS or not. Any prospective AIDS vaccine will have to undergo animal testing first. But the only test animals that can be infected with AIDS are chimpanzees and certain species of gibbon apes. Unfortunately, chimpanzees, the best test animals, are both extremely rare and extremely expensive, and many people object violently to using them for "inhumane" medical experiments. Dr. Gallo underscores this problem: "To do the vaccine studies I would like to do over the next two years I need seventy-five chimps, but I will be lucky to get two or three. So let's say I have ten *candidate* vaccines to test. Without enough chimps the research will take six years instead of six months. It is conceivable that we may already have an effective vaccine, but we'll never know unless we can get enough chimps to fine-tune different doses of different compounds." He adds, "Nobody is to blame. It's just that twenty-five years ago nobody, including me, had the foresight to begin chimpanzee breeding programs to provide for today's research needs."*

Obviously all of these problems have to be solved

---

*Gallo, R. C.: Grand Rounds interview with Dennis L. Breo. *American Medical News,* December 4, 1987.

before a vaccine can possibly be available. There is one bright side of the picture, however: a successful vaccine has been developed against the feline leukemia virus, another retrovirus that causes an AIDS-like disease in cats. Many workers are convinced that if that vaccine could be made to work against that virus, a vaccine against AIDS can be made to work, too—sooner or later.

Even if such a vaccine were available today and widely used, however, it could not have the immediate, dramatic impact on the occurrence of AIDS that the polio vaccine had on the occurrence of polio, simply because of the nature of the AIDS illness. We know that a new AIDS vaccine will have no effect on the virus already present in the bodies of infected people who have not yet developed any symptoms. Vaccines don't cure already-infected people, they merely prevent new infection from occurring. So even if a vaccine were available today and were given to everyone tomorrow, a multitude of people already infected will go right ahead and develop symptoms two or three or eight years in the future, and some of them will go on to develop full-blown AIDS still later on. We wouldn't see much impact of a new vaccine on the incidence of new AIDS infections for as much as four or five years, or more. In short, a vaccine is certainly a real hope for the future, but it isn't an answer to the AIDS problem today, or tomorrow either.

A NEW HIV?

Every day brings new discoveries about AIDS infection, HIV, and other retroviruses as well. For example, in the search for the AIDS virus, a related but different retrovirus called HTLV-I was discovered to cause a rare form of blood cancer or leukemia in humans. At that time this virus was found only in southern Japan and in the Caribbean Islands. Recently, however, HTLV-I has been detected in some donor blood in the New York area, missed by HIV screening because HIV antibody tests don't pick up HTLV-I antibodies.

Possibly more ominous, a second HIV virus, called HIV-2, has made an appearance in the United States. This close cousin to the HIV retrovirus has previously accounted for AIDS cases mainly in Central Africa— but now at least one AIDS patient in the New York-New Jersey area has been found to have HIV-2 antibodies, not the expected HIV antibodies. No one yet knows if HIV-2 is a mutation of the original HIV or a separate retrovirus present all along, and no one yet knows if it will spread to the extent that the original HIV is spreading. It is just one more worry and complication in this already worrisome and complicated epidemic.

Meanwhile, AIDS is raising some immense social problems to which nobody has any good solutions. We mentioned some of these earlier in regard to HIV antibody testing. But other problems are also already among us, or looming up in the future. One such problem is the irrational public fear, bordering on panic in some places, engendered by the disease. In this connection, for example, the city of Arcadia, Florida, will go down in medical history for one of the ugliest incidents in recent times. A family with two hemophilic boys, both afflicted with AIDS, tried to enter the children in school there. The boys were first treated like lepers and then thrown out of school altogether as a result of public pressure. The whole family was threatened, and when they sought police protection and enforcement of their legal rights, they received neither. Unsatisfied with all this, the good people of Arcadia, Florida, then burned them out of their home in a frenzy of ignorant, unreasoning fear, forcing them to flee for their lives.

Fortunately, other communities have met such problems with common humanity and grace. But other kinds of fears keep cropping up. Blood banks are having trouble finding enough blood donors because of a widespread false idea that a person can contract AIDS by *donating* blood. Of course this is plain silly—*there is no way it could happen*—but this is what people think just the same. Some hospitals are unwilling, on one pretext or another, to accept AIDS patients, and some doctors refuse to treat them despite a public policy statement by the American Medical Association declaring it unethical for doctors to refuse such care. Even in the matter of public education about AIDS there is conflict. Parents, even whole communities, object to explicit sexual education for their children to make them more aware of what AIDS is about and how it is transmitted, and some churches and communities object, for example, to discussions of condom use as protection for sexually active young people.

Finally, there is one overriding problem that won't go away—the staggering cost of medical care for this disease. Already it is a crushing financial burden for the more than 50,000 people with full-blown AIDS and the many more with AIDS-Related Complex. With estimates of over 200,000 cases of full-blown AIDS by the early 1990s, we are talking about a truly ghastly national financial burden. Many victims have no resources at all to pay for their care. More and more health insurance plans are refusing to cover AIDS-related costs, or even to insure applicants who test HIV-positive at all. So who is going to pay all the bills? Only those who contract the disease? Only those few patients who are rich? Or society as a whole? These questions have barely been raised, much less answered.

THE OUTLOOK
FOR THE FUTURE

For today and tomorrow the outlook for AIDS obviously isn't very cheerful. But for people with a philosophical attitude, there really is a long-term silver lining that may ultimately appear from our experience with this terrible disease and the massive research effort that it has engendered. In order to see this silver lining, you have to have the kind of mind that can recognize that the worldwide disaster that once destroyed all the dinosaurs (which was certainly a terrible thing for the dinosaurs) was also the upheaval that paved the way on this planet for the later rise of the mammals and ultimately of human beings. Without that worldwide disaster, whatever it was, we might still have a world full of dinosaurs and no human beings.

With regard to the AIDS virus and the devastating trouble it can cause, people with philosophic minds point out that in tracking down, identifying, and learning about the behavior of this newly arrived virus, we may end up with an enormously powerful and valuable body of knowledge about the nature and behavior of viruses in general, and about their role in contributing to other human diseases even more disastrous than AIDS. Remember for a moment that this new virus is a *retrovirus* —hitherto one of the most mysterious kinds of viruses ever encountered. Consider that HIV is very closely related to other retroviruses that we already know for certain are directly (and probably causally) related to various rare human cancers—human T-cell leukemia and hairy-cell leukemia, for example. We are just barely beginning to grasp exactly how such viruses, or other viruses, can actually work to cause healthy cells to become cancerous—and this understanding, once achieved, can advance us a long, long step in the direction of preventing cancers before they can start, rather than just fighting them down after they occur.

Almost certainly the forced research made necessary by the appearance of AIDS on the human scene will bring many more answers in the far broader area of human cancer. And a broader understanding of the inner genetic workings—the DNA and RNA behavior—of retroviruses and other viruses will also bring with it a broader understanding of the inner genetic workings of human cells, and will provide us with keys to the prevention, treatment, or cure of dozens of other gene-related diseases in humans.

There may be other benefits as well. AIDS is making incredible demands on every segment of our society, social demands as well as scientific ones. As this epidemic runs its course we are learning much about ourselves as a society as we respond to its challenge. How we behave as civilized human beings in the face of trial will be tested again and again. Our ability to be guided by reason rather than panic, our compassion toward others in terrible trouble, our willingness to make necessary changes in the way we live—all will be called to task. Only time will tell how we as a society will measure up.

The epidemic of AIDS that is going on right now is a terrible thing, and we can't at this time see the end to it. The best we can do, for the time being, is seek to protect ourselves through defensive living. But it is encouraging to realize that the long-term payoff in terms of expanded knowledge can be very great indeed. We can be certain that sooner or later AIDS will be effectively stopped—but the expanded knowledge we gain in the meantime will go on forever.

Acyclovir—an antiviral drug that helps suppress activity of the herpes simplex viruses, and may prove useful, in combination with AZT, in treating AIDS.

Acquired immune deficiency syndrome (AIDS)—a disease acquired by infection with a virus that attacks lymph cells and causes an immune deficiency, a breakdown in the body's protective immune system, leading to a syndrome or collection of disabling symptoms and resulting in death in a high percentage of cases.

AIDS-Related Complex (ARC)—a group or complex of troubling symptoms that may appear at some time after a person has been infected by the AIDS virus but which do not include the disabling symptoms of full-blown AIDS. AIDS experts believe that ARC is a first stage of symptoms due to infection with the AIDS virus and that most persons with ARC will eventually develop full-blown AIDS.

Alpha-interferon—a natural body protein that may have some antiviral activity in the body to help combat the AIDS virus HIV.

Amino acid—a fragment of protein that, combined with many others, goes to make up a DNA molecule.

Antibodies—special proteins produced by the body's immune system to circulate in the blood stream and fight off a foreign protein or antigen such as a virus.

AZT (azidothymidine)—an antiviral drug approved by the Food and Drug Administration (FDA) in 1987 for treatment of AIDS. The drug does not cure AIDS but can suppress the virus's activity for a while and thus prolong the lives of many AIDS patients. Its use is limited because of its high toxicity to healthy cells. AZT has now been renamed *zidovudine* and sold under the trade name Retrovir, but it's all the same drug.

B-cells—lymphocytes that originate in the bone marrow and are responsible for the production of protective antibodies.

Bacteria—one-celled plantlike organisms that in some cases can cause infections.

Candidiasis (thrush)—an infection, often affecting the mouth or throat, caused by the yeast known as *Candida albicans.*

Carriers—individuals who have recovered from an infection—or have not yet developed symptoms of an infection, in the case of AIDS—but still carry the live, infective organism in their bodies and can therefore transmit the infection to other people.

Enzyme—special protein substances that exist in all living organisms from humans to viruses and act to speed up or slow down biochemical reactions.

Hepatitis B—a serious virus infection of the liver that is transmitted by contact with contaminated blood or hypodermic needles, or by sexual contact. Some people who recover from hepatitis B continue to carry the live virus in their bodies and transmit it to others.

Human immunodeficiency virus (HIV)—the name scientists give to the AIDS virus today.

Human T-cell lymphotropic virus (HTLV)—one of a group or family of similar viruses that, upon invading the body, seek out and attack lymphocytes. HTLV-I and HTLV-II cause rare forms of leukemia in humans. HTLV-III, the virus found to be the cause of AIDS, attacks lymphocytes and causes the slow destruction of the body's immune system. It is now known as *human immunodeficiency virus* or HIV.

Immune deficient—a condition in which some part of the body's protective immune system is not working properly and thus fails to provide normal immune protection.

Incubation period—the interval from the time a virus first invades a host cell to the time when it has successfully forced the host cell to produce more virus particles and release them into the bloodstream.

Interleukin 2—a naturally formed body protein that may have some antiviral activity in the body to help combat the AIDS virus (HIV).

Kaposi's sarcoma—a cancer of blood vessels in the skin, ordinarily appearing only rarely among elderly people but commonly occurring in much younger people who have AIDS.

Latent period—the interval from the time an infecting virus is being reproduced or replicated in its host cells and the time symptoms of the infection begin to appear.

Leukemias—cancers in which various kinds of white blood cells in the bloodstream or bone marrow begin growing and reproducing wildly, beyond normal body control. Leukemias are often called "blood cancers."

Lymphadenopathy—an abnormal swelling of the lymph glands.

Lymphadenopathy-associated virus (LAV)—a virus first isolated in France from people with lymphadenopathy syndrome at about the same time as HTLV-III virus was first identified in people with AIDS. Later the LAV and the HTLV-III viruses were found to be virtually identical and are now called human immunodeficiency virus or HIV.

Lymphadenopathy syndrome (LAS)—a group of symptoms including fever, weight loss, and swelling of lymph glands over a prolonged period of time, believed to be an early manifestation of infection with the AIDS virus. These symptoms are now included in a wider group of pre-AIDS symptoms known as *AIDS-Related Complex* or *ARC.*

Lymph glands (lymph nodes)—small glandlike clusters of lymphocytes located in the neck, under the arms, in the groin, in the abdomen, or in other parts of the body.

Lymphocytes—small white blood cells formed in the bone marrow and lymph nodes which form the backbone of the body's protective immune system.

Lymphocytic leukemia—a leukemia involving wild growth or proliferation of lymphocytes.

Lymphomas—solid, enlarging cancers of the lymph glands or other lymph tissues.

Lymphotropic—drawn to, or seeking, lymph cells. A lymphotropic virus is one that seeks out lymphocytes *in particular* as its host cells.

Macrophages—large white blood cells that engulf and digest invading bacteria or virus particles. Certain macrophages are also called *monocytes.*

Microörganisms—life forms around us that are so tiny they can only be seen with microscopes.

Mutation—a change in an organism's genetic material, so that future generations are slightly different from earlier generations.

Neurotropic—drawn to, or seeking nerve cells in the brain or nervous system.

Nucleic acid—the genetic material inside living cells or viruses, in the form of deoxyribonucleic acid (DNA) or ribonucleic acid (RNA).

Opportunistic infections—infections that occur in people who have immune deficiencies, usually caused by organisms that could not survive in the presence of a normal, healthy immune system.

Pneumocystis carinii—a protozoan organism that normally is suppressed by the immune system when it invades the human body. In persons with AIDS, these organisms can cause a fast-moving, often fatal, *Pneumocystis carinii* pneumonia or PCP.

Precursor cells—cells that produce other kinds of cells. Precursor cells in the bone marrow produce lymphocytes that are released to circulate in the blood.

Protozoans—single-celled animal-like microorganisms, some of which can produce infections in humans.

Retroviruses—extremely primitive viruses that contain their genetic material in the form of RNA rather than DNA. These viruses contain a special enzyme, reverse transcriptase, that makes it possible for them to be reproduced in an infected host cell.

Reverse transcriptase—an enzyme present in all retroviruses, necessary for their reproduction.

Syndrome—a characteristic collection or pattern of symptoms or signs.

T-cells—lymphocytes that are acted upon by hormones in the thymus gland before they reach the bloodstream. Some groups of T-cells help control how quickly or slowly antibodies are produced by the B-cells.

T-helper cells (T-helper lymphocytes or T4 cells)—T-cells that help speed up the production of antibodies by the B-cells.

T-suppressor cells (T-suppressor lymphocytes or T8 cells)—T-cells that suppress or slow down the production of antibodies by the B-cells.

Yeast—a kind of fungus often associated with fermentation of sugar in fruit juices, bread doughs, etc. Some yeasts, such as *Candida albicans,* can cause infections in humans.

Zidovudine—the new and scientifically correct name for AZT or Azidothymidine.

Page numbers in *italics* refer to illustrations.